PRAYERS
to the
HOLY
SPIRIT

Power *and* Light
for Your Life

PRAYERS
to the
HOLY
SPIRIT

Power *and* Light
for Your Life

BERT GHEZZI

Published by The Word Among Us Press
7115 Guilford Drive
Frederick Maryland 21704
www.wau.org
All rights reserved

21 20 19 18 17   3 4 5 6 7

ISBN: 978-1-59325-252-6
eISBN: 978-1-59325-456-8

Cover design by Koechel Peterson & Associates

Made and printed in the United States of America

Library of Congress Control Number: 2014930871

Books by Bert Ghezzi

Voices of the Saints

The Saints Devotional Bible

The Power of Daily Prayer

Discover Christ (with Dave Nodar)

Breakfast with Benedict (compiler/editor)

Everyday Encounters with God
(with Benedict Groeschel, CFR)

Saints at Heart

Living the Sacraments

The Sign of the Cross

Mystics and Miracles

Getting Free

Contents

◇◇◇◇◇◇◇◇◇◇◇◇◇

Introduction / 11

1. Experiencing the Spirit / 16

2. Born of Water and the Spirit / 18

3. "Re-Peopling" the Earth / 20

4. The Holy Spirit Is a Someone / 22

5. Finding Your Service / 24

6. The Art Restorer / 26

7. Behavior Modification / 28

8. Answers of the Spirit / 30

9. Joy Trumps Gloom / 32

10. The Rain of God / 34

11. Befriending the Poor / 36

12. Seven Graces / 38

13. Praying in the Presence / 40

14. Living the Truth / 42

15. The Font of Light / 44

16. Standing Your Ground / 46

17. Gifted for Others / 48

18. Desires of the Heart / 50

19. Filled with Love / 52

20. Zeal for Evangelization / 54

21. Merciful Fathers / 56

22. Like the Wind / 58

23. The New Resident / 60

24. Real Food / 62

25. Inconvenient Holiness / 64

26. Help on the Way / 66

27. Ladies' Night / 68

28. The Prayer Starter / 70

29. Doing the Wise Thing / 72

30. Occasions of Grace / 74

31. Behaving Patiently / 76

32. Getting Free / 78

33. The Humble Healer / 80

34. Becoming a Saint / 82

35. Spirit-Led Service / 84

36. An Open Heart / 86

37. A Little Miracle / 88

38. The Holy Spirit *and* Us / 90

39. No Mere Mortals / 92

40. Strengthened for Suffering / 94

41. Making Peace / 96

42. Healing Graces / 98

43. The Water of Life / 100

44. The Teacher of Everything / 102

45. An Excess of Compassion / 104

46. Mary Opens Us to the Spirit / 106

47. Words of Encouragement / 108

48. Spiritual Equilibrium/ 110

49. Reality Checks / 112

50. Speaking from Experience / 114

51. The Spirit Is In You / 116

52. Inspired Repartee / 118

53. Divine Mysteries / 120

54. A Generous Spirit / 122

55. Praying in Tongues / 124

56. Encouraging Words / 126

57. Another Advocate / 128

58. Gifted to Serve / 130

59. The Spirit's Priorities / 132

60. Getting Self under Control / 134

61. The Radiance of the Spirit / 136

62. Everyday Courage / 138

63. A Gift of Fear / 140

64. A Kiss of Kindness / 142
65. The Four Essential Keys / 144
66. Using Your Gifts Wisely / 146
67. Humility's Fruit / 148
68. Lifelong Learning / 150
69. The Loop of Grace / 152
70. Living Sacrifices / 154
71. Keeping the Peace / 156
72. Serving with Joy / 158
73. Probing God's Mind / 160
74. Loving Like God / 162
75. The Supreme Desire / 164
    Prayers to the Holy Spirit / 166
    Recommended Resources / 172
    Acknowledgments / 173
    Endnotes / 174

Introduction

◇◇◇◇◇◇◇◇◇◇◇◇◇◇◇◇◇◇◇◇◇◇

The Spirit of God has made a home in you.
—Romans 8:9, NJB

Welcome to *Prayers to the Holy Spirit: Power and Light for Your Life*, a little book that offers you a big opportunity to give yourself more fully to the Lord. Here you will find reflections and prayers designed to open you to renewing your life in the Spirit.

The Holy Spirit came to dwell in you when you became a Christian and received the sacraments of initiation—Baptism, Confirmation, and the Eucharist. From that time he has worked within you, enlightening you, forming you as a Christian, empowering you with gifts, and more. I like to describe him as the Holy Spirit the Worker, who comes to us with his toolbox full of blessings, graces, and gifts. Here are some of his workings, which this book highlights:

❖ The Holy Spirit is the Giver of Life. He breathed life into the first creation and he animates the new creation, which is the body of Christ, the Church.

❖ The Holy Spirit has made his home in us, establishing each of us as his temple and making us holy.

❖ The Holy Spirit enlightens our minds, unpacking for us the teachings of Jesus and the Church.

❖ The Holy Spirit is our Advocate, which means that he defends us against whatever threatens us, counsels us when we're troubled or confused, and intercedes for us, especially when we don't know how to pray.

❖ The Holy Spirit transforms us, making us more like Christ. He does this by giving us gifts that illumine our minds—wisdom, knowledge, understanding, and counsel—and gifts that

make our hearts glow with love—piety, fortitude, and reverence.

❖ The Holy Spirit renews us in the Lord's image
by planting in us the seeds of the fruit of the
Spirit, which prompt us to conduct ourselves as
Jesus would.

❖ The Holy Spirit empowers each of us with charismatic gifts that equip us to fulfill our mission
to bring others to Christ and to the Church.

Each of the seventy-five chapters of *Prayers to the
Holy Spirit* begins with a brief **Scripture text** and a
reflection on one or more of these workings of the
Spirit. You will find meditations on Scripture, mini-
teachings from Church Fathers and theologians,
examples from the lives of saints and contemporary
Catholics, and stories from my own experience.

An **application** follows each reflection, which shows
you how to respond to the Holy Spirit. You will see

what you must do to relate the message of the reflection to your life.

Then you will find a **"May you" blessing,** which commends you to the Lord and asks for graces to help you appropriate the Spirit's gifts or participate in his work.

Finally, each chapter ends with a **prayer starter,** which you can use to launch meditation, petition, thanksgiving, or adoration.

I invite you to approach your reading of *Prayers to the Holy Spirit* with faith—and not just with the faith that believes the truth of doctrines, nor merely the daily faith that expresses your trust in God. Rather, you should approach the Lord with expectant faith— a faith that counts on God to act. According to what Jesus says in the Gospel of Luke, when we ask the Lord for an outpouring of the Spirit, we can expect to receive him:

"So I say to you: Ask, and it will be given to you; search, and you will find; knock, and the door will be opened to you. For everyone who asks receives; everyone who searches finds; everyone who knocks will have the door opened. What father among you, if his son asked for a fish, would hand him a snake? Or if he asked for an egg, hand him a scorpion? If you then, evil as you are, know how to give your children what is good, how much more will the heavenly Father give the Holy Spirit to those who ask him!" (Luke 11:9-13, NJB)

So may you approach the Lord expecting him to do what he promises. May you meet the Holy Spirit afresh in these pages. And with each chapter, may you be flooded with love for the Lord and feel the power and light of his Spirit.

Experiencing the Spirit

"You will receive power when the holy Spirit comes upon you, and you will be my witnesses . . . to the ends of the earth."
—*Acts 1:8*

Just before Jesus ascended to his Father, he made a striking promise to his disciples. He told them that they could expect to have a powerful experience of the Holy Spirit. He said that empowered by the Spirit, they would be equipped to bear witness to him throughout the earth. Jesus intended his promise of the Holy Spirit to extend to all of his disciples, including those of the twenty-first century. That means that today's Christians should have a dual expectation: we should expect to experience the Holy Spirit's power in our lives, and we should expect him to work through us to draw others to Christ and his Church.

You received the Holy Spirit when you were baptized and confirmed. He really came into your life, but you may not have experienced his presence or power. If that's the case, you should recommit your life to Jesus. Tell him that you give yourself to him and want him to release the Holy Spirit in you so fully that you can tell he is at work in you.

> May you come to receive the fullness of the Spirit, experience his presence and power, and by his grace become more effective in sharing the Good News.

Lord Jesus, I believe that you are the Son of God and that you gave your life for me. I commit my life to you and ask you to fill me afresh with the Holy Spirit and his gifts.

Born of Water and the Spirit

"Amen, amen, I say to you, no one can enter the kingdom of God without being born of water and Spirit."
—John 3:5

St. Basil the Great (ca. 329–378) explains what it means to be born of water and the Spirit:

There is in baptism an image both of death and of life, the water being the symbol of death, the Spirit giving the pledge of life. The association of water and the Spirit is explained by the two-fold purpose of baptism: . . . to destroy sin in us so that it could never again give birth to death, and to enable us to live by the Spirit and so win the reward of holiness. The water into which the body enters as into a tomb symbolizes death; the Spirit instills into us his life-giving power.

. . . We die in the water and come to life again through the Spirit.[1]

We often think of Baptism as a cleansing of our souls from sin. But Baptism is much more. In Baptism we die by drowning in the water and we rise to new life in the Spirit. So we can pray for a renewal of our baptismal graces, rejoicing in our death to sin and in our new life of holiness in the Spirit.

May seeing Baptism as a dying and a rising to life in the Spirit be a source of faith, hope, and love for you, and may the Spirit renew in you the regenerative power of your baptism.

O Holy Spirit, thank you for my death to sin in the waters of Baptism and for my new life in you. Renew in me the graces of my baptism, and help me to grow in holiness.

"Re-Peopling" the Earth

Send forth your spirit, they are created /
and you renew the face of the earth.
—*Psalm 104:30*

The liturgy of the Easter Vigil adapts this verse and makes it a plea: "Lord, send out your Spirit, and renew the face of the earth." The Spirit of God gives life to all creatures—animals, birds, fish, and human beings. And in a broader sense, when we are baptized, he gives us new life, a share in his own divine life. For this reason, a friend of mine once suggested that we should read the verse as "you re-people the face of the earth." He meant that the Spirit really changes us by elevating our nature and making us like Christ.

Maybe you don't feel as though the Holy Spirit has changed you, but he has. He has given you a supernatural life that makes you holy, that equips you to participate in the Eucharist and all the sacraments, that gives you the powers of faith, hope, and love for daily living—and more.

> May you begin every morning asking the Lord to send you his Spirit, and may you daily experience the newness of divine life that enables you to become more like Jesus.

Lord, I want to learn how to live the divine life you have given me. Please send the Holy Spirit to renew me and guide me in your ways.

The Holy Spirit Is a Someone

The grace of the Lord Jesus Christ and the
love of God and the fellowship of the
holy Spirit be with all of you.
—*2 Corinthians 13:13*

Catholic apologist Frank J. Sheed describes the relationship of the Holy Spirit to the Father and Son:

Father and Son love each other, with infinite intensity. What we could not know, if it were not revealed to us, is that they unite to express their love, and that expression is a third divine Person. . . . Each gives Himself wholly to the outpouring of His love for the Other, holding nothing back—indeed the very thought of holding back is ridiculous; if They give Themselves at all, They can give Themselves only totally—They possess nothing but Their totality! The uttered love of Father and Son is infinite, lacks no perfection that They have, is God, a Person, a Someone [—the Holy Spirit.][2]

The Holy Spirit has sometimes been called the "neglected" Person of the Trinity, the One who is "lonely." Perhaps because he is referred to as "Spirit," we find ourselves unable to imagine him, as we can Jesus. But we must rid ourselves of all such thoughts. Instead, we must embrace the truth that the Holy Spirit is God, a Person who fully shares life with the Father and the Son. Getting that straight prepares the way for us to come to know and love him more.

May you come to experience the Holy Spirit more personally and grasp more perfectly who he is and what he means for your life.

O Holy Spirit, I want to know you more and love you more. Draw me into your presence and reveal yourself to me.

Finding Your Service

◇◇◇◇◇◇◇◇◇◇◇◇◇◇◇◇◇◇◇◇◇◇◇◇◇◇◇◇◇◇◇◇◇◇◇

There are different kinds of spiritual gifts but the
same Spirit; . . . there are different workings but the
same God who produces all of them in everyone.
—1 Corinthians 12:4,6

Once during an interview, Pope St. John XXIII was
asked whether being pope kept him awake at night.
He replied, "Every night before I go to sleep, I kneel
down and pray this simple prayer: 'Dear God, it's
your Church. I'm going to bed.'" The pope understood that the Holy Spirit was wholly responsible for
the Church's life and that the Spirit had equipped him
to share in the work. The same holds true for us. The
Holy Spirit engages us to serve with him in caring for
the Church. He provides spiritual gifts that empower
us for our service (1 Corinthians 12:7-11). For example, to one he gives wisdom, which is inspired practical advice or understanding of a Christian truth. To
another, knowledge, which is spiritual insight into

a situation or a direction to act in a certain way. To some he gives faith, miracles, healing, prophecy, discernment, or other unnamed gifts.

Scripture presents two truths that many Christians fail to grasp. First, the Lord gives gifts of service to every Christian, "distributing them individually to *each person* as he wishes" (1 Corinthians 12:11, emphasis added). Second, the Lord wants us to seek our spiritual gifts by praying (12:31) and by exploring possible services.

> May you discover all the ways the Holy Spirit wants you to join his work. May you enjoy exercising your spiritual gifts to build up the body of Christ.

Holy Spirit, . . . / giver of gifts limitless, / come and touch our hearts today. / . . . As your promise we believe, / make us ready to receive / gifts from your unbounded store. (Veni Sancte Spiritus)

The Art Restorer

All of us, gazing with unveiled face on
the glory of the Lord, are being transformed into
the same image from glory to glory, as from the
Lord who is the Spirit.
—2 Corinthians 3:18

St. Gregory of Nyssa (ca. 330–395) said that the Lord
is an artist who paints us as portraits in his own
image. For colors he uses virtues to make us resemble his own beauty. With divine brushstrokes, he portrays us with purity, freedom from passion, integrity,
blessedness, alienation from all evil, and all the spiritual powers that form us in his likeness. But by every
honest assessment, our sinfulness has damaged that
image. To repair it and bring us back to our original
beauty, the Holy Spirit comes to us in the sacraments
as an "art restorer." He frees us from our sin, and he

renews our likeness to God by transforming us from one degree of glory to another.[3]

We need to look in the mirror of Scripture to assess the damage our sinful behavior has done to the image of God in which we are created. Then we must ask the Holy Spirit, the divine Art Restorer, to remove dark layers from the portrait and brighten us with virtues.

> May the Holy Spirit make you more and more like Jesus every day. May he restore in you the beauty of the divine image by prompting you to live a virtuous life.

Come, Holy Spirit. Show me my sins and their causes so that I may honestly admit and confess them. Then renew me in your image with virtues so that I can live a holy life.

Behavior Modification

The fruit of the Spirit is love, joy, peace,
patience, kindness, generosity, faithfulness,
gentleness, self-control.
—Galatians 5:22-23

Many Christians regard love, joy, peace, and the other fruit of the Spirit as feelings, and they are disappointed when they try to stir them up. However, St. Paul presents the fruit of the Spirit not as feelings ,but primarily as behaviors that replace the works of the flesh (Galatians 5:19-21.) For example, acts of love correct hateful conduct, peaceful initiatives calm fighting, patient behaviors replace angry outbursts, exercising self-control checks lustful acts, and so on. We receive these behaviors when we ask the Holy Spirit for the grace to conduct ourselves as Jesus would. Then we perform the actions that manifest the fruit of the Spirit. For example, to grow in love, we must do the loving thing in every situation, serving even someone we do not like. The Spirit will honor our repeating of this behavior by producing the fruit of love in us.

We recognize the works of the flesh in our lives and feel doomed to repeat them over and over. But we don't have to: the Holy Spirit brings us antidotes that we can use to break free of them.

> May you face evil inclinations and persistent sinful patterns by expecting the Holy Spirit to give you the grace to overcome them, and may you replace them with the fruit of the Spirit.

Come, Holy Spirit. Help me to see clearly the works of the flesh in my life. Give me the grace to replace my evil behaviors with the fruit of the Spirit.

Answers of the Spirit

◇◇◇◇◇◇◇◇◇◇◇◇◇◇◇◇◇◇◇◇◇◇◇◇◇◇◇◇◇◇◇◇◇◇◇◇◇◇

Bless the LORD, O my soul, / who heals
. . . / all your diseases.
—Psalm 103:2-3, RSV

My mother was a lovely and generous woman. However, she had a lifelong problem with anger, which affected her relationship with my two sisters. In traditional Italian families, daughters did not leave home until they were married. So when my sisters moved out after graduating from college, Mother sizzled over their decision and held it against them. Later, she was diagnosed with breast cancer, and my sisters and I gathered around her and asked the Holy Spirit to heal her. To our disappointment, she died within a year. But the Spirit gave our mother an unexpected healing: six months before her death, he cured her anger, and she spent many happy hours with her daughters.

You can create a relationship of trust with God the Holy Spirit so that when you ask him for anything, especially something "big" like a healing, you expect him to hear your prayer. But you must let God be God and give you the answer he chooses. Sometimes he says yes, and sometimes he says wait. And at other times, he says no—and that he has something better for you, as he did for my mother.

May the fruit of your daily prayer be a solid trust in the Holy Spirit and his goodness, and when you ask for something, may you remain open to his gracious answer.

O Holy Spirit, I place all my trust in you. I don't want to come to you with a wobbly faith, so I ask you to fill me with confidence. Help me to embrace with joy whatever answers you give to my petitions.

Joy Trumps Gloom

<><><><><><><><><><><><><><><><><><><><><>

Rejoice in the Lord always.
I shall say it again: rejoice!
—*Philippians 4:4*

I love Blessed Pier-Giorgio Frassati (1901–1925) because he was so "normal." Surrounded by a circle of friends, he was an athlete, a mountain climber, the life of every party, a practical joker, and a lover of poetry. He was also a servant of the poor and marginalized, a man of prayer, a political organizer, and a saint. Pier-Giorgio pursued his life with enthusiasm.

However, he was profoundly saddened by the daily tension generated by the deteriorating marriage of his parents. No one would have noticed his unhappiness because he replaced it with joy, practicing it as a fruit of the Spirit. "Down with all melancholy," he said. "That should never be found except in the heart which has lost faith. I am joyful. . . . Gloom should be banished from the Christian soul."[4] So, led by the Spirit, Pier-Giorgio behaved joyfully in all circumstances.

St. Paul challenges us to rejoice. That he commands joy tells us that it is more something that we decide to do than a feeling we try to stir up. The Holy Spirit enables us to substitute joyful behaviors for gloomy ones.

> May you imitate Blessed Pier-Giorgio and banish every trace of gloom from your soul, and may you allow the Holy Spirit to empower you to obey St. Paul's command to rejoice.

O Holy Spirit, sometimes when I survey the circumstances of my life, I feel sad. I want to rejoice always, but I don't always know how. Give me the grace to banish gloom from my soul, and prompt me with ways to do it.

The Rain of God

<><><><><><><><><><><><><><><><><><><>

"The water I shall give will become in him a spring
of water welling up to eternal life."
—*John 4:14*

St. Cyril of Jerusalem (ca. 315–386) explains why
Jesus used water as an image for the grace of the Spirit:

Water comes down from heaven as rain, and
although it is always the same in itself, it produces many different effects, one in the palm
tree, another in the vine, and so on. . . . In the
same way, the Holy Spirit, whose nature is
always the same, . . . apportions grace to each
person as he wills. . . . [He] makes one man
a teacher of divine truth, inspires another to
prophesy, gives another the power of casting
out devils, enables another to interpret holy
Scripture. The Spirit strengthens one man's self-
control, shows another how to help the poor,

teaches another to fast and lead a life of ascet-
icism, . . . trains another for martyrdom. His
action is different in different people, but the
Spirit himself is always the same.[5]

Jesus told the Samaritan woman to ask for living
water that would become a spring welling up in her
to eternal life. Just as the earth needs rain to enliven
plants and trees, you need the Holy Spirit to flood
your being with new life and to strengthen you with
his gifts.

May you experience the Spirit you received in
Baptism as a spring welling up within you. May
you expect him to cleanse you, nourish you,
and give you whatever gifts he wants to give.

Come, Holy Spirit. Flood my being with your presence.
Come like the rain and drench me with your graces.
Flow in me, and let me experience your gentle power.

Befriending the Poor

*Pay no regard to social standing,
but meet humble people on their own terms.*
—Romans 12:16, NJB

When my friend Brandon was a university student, he had a strong, biblically-based concern for the poor. But one day he realized that he had no personal contact with poor people. So he went to a park, where he met Joe, a homeless man, and shared a burger with him. Over several months the two became friends. This friendship with Joe had a transforming effect on Brandon. He is now an advocate for befriending marginalized people. For example, he has headed up our parish's social justice commission and has championed numerous efforts to help the needy. Looking at the fruit of Brandon's labors, I am sure I see the Holy Spirit at work in him.

We have compassionate feelings for the poor and find it easy to be generous in giving to programs that serve them. But do we have any friendships with our poor neighbors? We must learn to imitate saints like Blessed Frédéric Ozanam, who regarded a personal visit with a poor family even more important than a gift of food.

May the Holy Spirit touch your heart with compassion and concern for the poor and marginalized, and may he give you opportunities to become friends with your neighbors in need.

I open my heart to you, O Holy Spirit, and ask you to fill me with love and compassion for the poor. Lead me into friendships with needy people, and show me how to serve them with kindness, sensitivity, and respect.

Seven Graces

<><><><><><><><><><><><><><><><><>

But a shoot shall sprout from the stump of Jesse . . . .
/ The spirit of the LORD shall rest upon him.
—Isaiah 11:1-2

Jesus fulfilled Isaiah's prophecy that the Spirit and his gifts would rest fully on a descendant of David. The Church understands that the Spirit and his gifts rest upon all of us who become members of the body of Christ, the Church. In the Sacrament of Confirmation, the Spirit gives us seven gifts. Four gifts enlighten our minds—wisdom, knowledge, understanding, and counsel; three strengthen our hearts—fortitude, piety, and fear of the Lord (Isaiah 11:2-3).[6] These gifts work as actual graces that prompt us to put virtues into practice (*Catechism of the Catholic Church*, 1831). Wisdom, for example, informs our will about right courses of action. Fortitude stirs our hearts to resist evil or stand up for the truth. These useful gifts help us to respond to the Church's universal call to holiness.

We need all the help we can get to live a holy life every day. Aided by the Spirit's gifts, we can conform our behavior to Jesus' formidable commands that we love God above all and love others as he loves us.

May you activate the gifts of the Spirit by faith, and may you use them to make right choices to do the loving thing in all circumstances.

Come, Creator Spirit . . . . / You who are sev'nfold in your grace, / Finger of God's right hand, / his promise, teaching all of us / to speak and understand. (Veni Creator Spiritus)

Praying in the Presence

<><><><><><><><><><><><><><><><><><><><><><><><><><><>

*With all prayer and supplication, pray at every
opportunity in the Spirit.*
—Ephesians 6:18

We remember Dorothy Day for her tireless service
of the poor, but we must also remember her faithfulness in prayer. Dorothy believed that to "pray without ceasing" (1 Thessalonians 5:17) meant dwell-
ing in the Lord's presence as she pursued her service. Busy with writing about social justice and doing
the works of mercy, Dorothy was never too busy to
skip prayer. She allowed the prayer of Christ to flow
through her by worshipping at daily Mass and praying a layperson's version of the Liturgy of the Hours.
Dorothy often took a break to visit the Blessed Sacrament to pray for the many needy people on her
intercessory list. Long before *lectio divina* became
popular, she used the movements of that prayerful

approach to Scripture. Most of all, Dorothy's faithful prayer opened her to the leadings of the Holy Spirit.

We are very busy people and easily find reasons not to take time to pray. But if we want to live as faithful disciples, like Dorothy Day we must dwell in the Lord's presence by building prayer into our daily routine.

May you find ways of joining Christ's prayer by opening your heart to him throughout the day, and as you pray, may you listen for the Holy Spirit's leadings.

Holy Spirit, Truth divine, / dawn upon this soul of mine; / Word of God and inward light, / wake my spirit; clear my sight. (from an 1864 hymn by Samuel Longfellow)

Living the Truth

◇◇◇◇◇◇◇◇◇◇◇◇◇◇◇◇◇◇◇◇◇

"But when he comes, the Spirit of truth,
he will guide you to all truth."
—*John 16:13*

Have you ever wondered why Jesus did not write a book that would tell us exactly what he wanted us to believe and do? He may have had other reasons not to write, but mainly, I think, he wanted us to learn to freely choose to follow him. So instead of writing a book, he left us the Holy Spirit, who would guide us to live by the truth.

The Holy Spirit has given us God's living word in Scripture and Tradition. These inspired dual sources of Christ's teaching offer us direction for our thoughts and actions. The Holy Spirit unfolds in them eternal truths about God and his creation. Through the leadership and instruction of popes, bishops, and saints, he shows us how to live according to Jesus' way.

May you find your life's direction in the living word of God, and may you follow the Spirit's leadings as you walk along the way he maps out for you.

Reveal to me, O Holy Spirit, what I need to know and do in order to live by the truths of Christ. With all my being, I want you to fill my thoughts with your wisdom and my heart with your love.

The Font of Light

×××××××××××××××××××××××××××××××

"But you know [the Spirit of truth], because it remains with you, and will be in you."
—*John 14:17*

St. Hilary (ca. 300–368) explains how the Holy Spirit enlightens our minds:

We receive the Spirit of truth so that we can know the things of God. . . . Consider how useless the faculties of the human body would become if they were denied their exercise. Our eyes cannot fulfill their task without light, either natural or artificial; our ears cannot react without sound vibrations. . . . Not that these senses would lose their nature if they were not used; rather, they demand objects of experience in order to function. It is the same with the human soul. Unless it absorbs the gift of the Spirit through faith, the mind has the ability to know God but lacks the light necessary for that knowledge.[7]

The Holy Spirit is with you and in you to give you the capacity to know God. You just have to flip the switch to let his light shine in your mind and heart. That switch is faith—a faith that expects the Holy Spirit to increase your knowledge and experience of the Father and the Son.

May you never be satisfied with shadowy religious knowledge but always seek the bright light of the Holy Spirit.

Holy Spirit, font of light, / focus of God's glory bright, / shed on us a shining ray. (Veni Sancte Spiritus)

Standing Your Ground

*The spirit of the LORD shall rest upon him: /
a spirit of . . . strength.*
—Isaiah 11:2

The Jesuit priest St. Roque Gonzalez (1576–1628)
dedicated his life to caring for the Guarani, a nomadic
Indian tribe of Paraguay. He loved them, and for
two decades, he labored and sacrificed to improve
their lives materially and spiritually. Roque built village communities where the Guarani learned new
and healthier ways of living. He protected them by
excluding from the villages the Spanish landowners
who wanted to enslave them. He also refused to hear
the confessions of landowners who would not repent
of their hostile actions toward the Guarani. I believe
the Holy Spirit gave St. Roque the gift of strength,
sometimes called "fortitude," to equip him to stand
his ground.

You probably will never have to oppose forces as powerful as the ones St. Roque withstood, but you will certainly find yourself in situations in which you will need a spiritual burst of fortitude to help you stand your ground.

> May you find the spiritual strength to stand up for what's right. May the Holy Spirit galvanize your will to resist evil with the same gift of fortitude that equipped St. Roque.

Strengthen me, O Holy Spirit, with the fortitude to withstand evil, to resist sin, and to do the right and loving thing in every circumstance. Examine my heart, and fortify any weakness you may discover there.

Gifted for Others

xxxxxxxxxxxxxxxxxxxxxxxxxxxxxxxxxx

His mother said to the servers,
"Do whatever he tells you."
—John 2:5

My first job was teaching at a state college. One day I walked into class and sensed the Holy Spirit saying that he wanted me to tell Tom, one of my students, that God loved him and wanted him to come to know him. Tom came to my office three times before I had the courage to do what the Spirit had told me to do. But when I finally did, Tom responded with eager faith. Over the next year, he gave his life fully to Christ. He spent the next thirty years as a leader in his church. The Lord could have spoken to Tom through anyone, but I was honored to have been chosen to tell him of God's love. I believe the Holy Spirit worked through me with the spiritual gift of knowledge, which is listed in 1 Corinthians 12:8.

Have you noticed the Holy Spirit prompting you to speak to someone or do something for him? Be watchful for his leadings, as he may be working through your thoughts for the good of another. He may be giving you the spiritual gift of knowledge to serve a friend, as he did for me with Tom.

May you always be alert to the workings of the Holy Spirit, and may you "do whatever he tells you," like the servers at the wedding of Cana.

Holy Spirit, I open the ears of my mind and heart for your leadings. Strengthen my will so that I may do whatever you tell me.

Desires of the Heart

◇◇◇◇◇◇◇◇◇◇◇◇◇◇◇◇◇◇◇◇◇◇◇◇◇◇◇◇◇◇◇◇

Now we have received not the spirit of the world,
but the Spirit which is from God, that we might
understand the gifts bestowed on us by God.
—1 Corinthians 2:12, RSV

From her youth, St. Katharine Drexel (1858–1955)
wanted to please God. So she sought his direction
by praying daily the *Veni Sancte Spiritus* (page 169–
70). She desired with all her heart to live a life of
quiet contemplation, but she began to experience a
conflicting desire when she and her sisters inherited
fourteen million dollars from their wealthy father.
Katharine wanted to give generously to ministries
that cared for Native and African Americans. But her
spiritual advisers directed her to serve these marginalized people herself. She founded a religious order
that in four decades established 145 missions and
twelve schools for Native Americans and fifty schools
for African Americans. After a heart attack in 1935,

she realized her first heart's desire and spent her last twenty years as a contemplative.

We sometimes deceive ourselves into thinking that our desires mislead us, but God may be putting desires in our hearts in order to show us what he wants us to do for him. I invite you to join me in praying to the Holy Spirit daily, seeking his direction as St. Katharine did.

> May you consider the desires of your heart, and may you have the grace to discern the Spirit's leadings and understand the gifts the Lord is giving you.

Give me the wisdom, O Holy Spirit, to test my heart's desires. Help me to pursue those that you are forming within me.

Filled with Love

◇◇◇◇◇◇◇◇◇◇◇◇◇◇◇◇◇◇◇◇◇◇◇◇◇

*Hope does not disappoint, because the love of God
has been poured out into our hearts through the holy
Spirit that has been given to us.*
—Romans 5:5

St. Paul makes the startling declaration that the Holy
Spirit pours the very love of God into our hearts. Just
think: the love that floods our beings is the same love
that burst forth from the Trinity and created the uni-
verse of 300 billion trillion stars. We don't grasp the
magnitude of this reality because we don't often feel
its presence. Yet God's love in us produces the hope
we need to endure afflictions, and this divine love
moves us to put serving God and others ahead of
serving ourselves.

None of us live free of suffering. We are afflicted with
financial pressures, illness, broken relationships, and

many other trials. How good to know that God's love strengthens us to endure every hardship!

> May you grow in awareness of the divine love that fills your heart. May you learn to allow that love to bear you up when suffering comes.

Thank you, Holy Spirit, for filling me with your love. Help me to recognize the presence of this divine gift and to rely on it when troubles afflict me.

Zeal for Evangelization

◇◇◇◇◇◇◇◇◇◇◇◇◇◇◇◇◇◇◇◇◇◇◇◇◇◇◇◇◇◇◇◇◇◇◇◇◇◇

Go, therefore, and make disciples of all nations.
—Matthew 28:19

By nature St. Anthony Mary Claret (1807–1870)
was an irrepressible evangelist. He recognized that
the Lord had made evangelization the purpose of
the Church. Thoroughly modern in his outlook and
methods, he spread the gospel creatively by establishing institutions that had wide-ranging impacts—
an international religious order, publishing ven-
tures, libraries, professional associations, schools,
museums, and cultural centers. In his lifetime, he
preached ten thousand sermons and published two
hundred books and pamphlets. St. Anthony founded
the Religious Library, which distributed five million
books and four million leaflets in two decades. He
also launched a religious order with his priest col-
laborators, which is now called the Claretians. And
the saint did one-on-one evangelism, speaking with

people in ways that invited them to conversion to Christ and his Church. Spirit-inspired zeal impelled St. Anthony, and he used his spiritual gifts effectively to proclaim the Good News.

Don't let the magnitude of St. Anthony's evangelistic accomplishments daunt you. Rather, let the Holy Spirit infect you with his zeal and his priority of evangelization. The Spirit gives each of us gifts for serving the Church's purpose—the winning of women and men to follow Christ.

> May you have an ardor for sharing your faith,
> and may you use your spiritual gifts creatively
> to draw others to Christ and the Church.

O Holy Spirit, stir in me an unquenchable desire to do the work of evangelization. Show me how to use all of my spiritual gifts to bring others to the Lord.

Merciful Fathers

"Be merciful, just as your Father is merciful."
—Luke 6:36

Once a friend called me aside and gave me some parental advice. "I have been observing the way you relate to your son," he said, "and if you don't let up on him, you are going to drive him away from you and from God." He showed me that I was holding my teenager to the highest standards in every area of his life. My friend urged me to lower my expectations in some matters, like dress and orderliness, and hold my son to the highest standard only in the areas of responsibility and morality. I believe the Holy Spirit was speaking through my friend, nudging me to be a merciful father to my son as the Lord has been a merciful Father to me. So I adjusted my expectations, and as a result, my son stayed closer to me and to God.

The Holy Spirit may be trying to get a word of correction to you, and there are many ways he may attempt to get your attention. One way might be to speak to you through a friend.

> May you listen carefully to your friends as they encourage and advise you. May you discern the voice of the Holy Spirit, the Counselor, in your conversations with them.

Holy Spirit, you are my Counselor. I want you to direct my life and keep me securely on the right path. Please guide me in all that I say and do. Help me to hear you speaking to me through my relatives and friends, and correct any flaws you see in the ways I relate to the people I love.

Like the Wind

✕✕✕✕✕✕✕✕✕✕✕✕✕✕✕✕✕✕✕

*"The wind blows where it wills, . . . but you do not
know where it comes from or where it goes; so it is
with everyone who is born of the Spirit."*
—John 3:8

St. Jane de Chantal (1572–1641) explains how the
Spirit changes us imperceptibly:

> When the Holy Spirit enters us, the course he
> follows is unknown. He is like the wind. It is
> enough to know that we have received him by
> the effects he produces every day and by feel-
> ing ourselves stronger than we were—without
> knowing how or when this grace came to us.
> Certainly, it can only have come as a result of
> our frequently offering our hearts to God. We
> do not see trees or human bodies growing, but
> afterwards we are astonished at seeing their
> increase. It is the same with souls. They advance

in the way of God, although they don't perceive it, provided that they faithfully respond to the lights and attractions of grace.[8]

Have you ever noticed that in small ways, you have changed for the better? Maybe you're listening better during prayer, or not losing it when little things go wrong. That means the Holy Spirit is working in you because you are faithfully giving yourself to God.

May you always offer your heart to God in prayer. And may you grow in holiness—imperceptibly—as you faithfully respond to the graces of the Holy Spirit.

Come, Creator Spirit, come / . . . O guide our minds with your blest light, / with love our hearts inflame; / and with your strength, which ne'er decays, / confirm our mortal frame. (Veni Creator Spiritus)

The New Resident

Do you not know that your body is a temple of the holy Spirit within you, whom you have from God, and that you are not your own?
—1 Corinthians 6:19

Like the Christians of Corinth, we are immersed in a sexually charged culture, rampant with temptation. Pornography, contraception, casual sex, marital infidelity, and more conspire to erode our moral sensibilities. St. Paul's words to our ancient forebearers still speak to us. He declares that our bodies do not belong to us. The Father ransomed us, body and soul, for the price of his Son's death. The Holy Spirit has claimed ownership by taking up residence in us, and as temples of the Spirit, we can resist temptation and walk in holiness.

Sexual temptation comes in degrees. For some, it may be merely a mild distraction; for others, a constant attraction; and for still others, a terrible compulsion. God made sexual desire good and built it into us, so sexual temptation is not going to go away. It's best to resist it by holding ourselves daily to the truth of St. Paul's teaching: our bodies do not belong to us but to the "new resident" who has made them his temple.

May you always have the wisdom and strength to walk through our sexually charged world, regarding your body as a temple of the Holy Spirit.

How good it is, O Holy Spirit, that you have come to make your home in me. Strengthen me deep within to maintain an upright conscience and to fight temptation.

Real Food

◇◇◇◇◇◇◇◇◇◇◇◇◇◇◇◇

"Whoever eats my flesh and drinks my blood
remains in me and I in him."
—*John 6:56*

When we worship at Mass, we participate in a re-pre-sentation of Jesus' eternal sacrifice. The Holy Spirit occasions this miracle by transforming bread and wine into the Lord's Body and Blood. In Eucharistic Prayer IV, the priest prays, "May this same Holy Spirit graciously sanctify these offerings, that they may become the Body and Blood of our Lord Jesus Christ for the celebration of this great mystery, which he himself left us as an eternal covenant."[9] Thus, the Holy Spirit makes Jesus really present among us, and with the priest, we join ourselves to Christ in his sacrifice, which unites us to the Father.

The real presence of Jesus in the Eucharist—Body, Blood, soul, and divinity—constitutes the very heart of the Catholic faith. The Second Vatican Council taught that the Eucharist is "the source and summit of the Christian life" (*Lumen Gentium*, 11). Jesus wants us to build our faith on this truth, for he said that unless we eat his Body and Blood, we will not have eternal life within us (John 6:53).

May the Holy Spirit deepen your understanding and experience of Jesus' real presence in the Eucharist. May he prompt you at Mass to offer yourself fully to the Father as you join Christ in his sacrifice.

Holy Spirit, I ask you to make me keenly aware and appreciative of Jesus' real presence in the Eucharist. I believe that you transform bread into his Body and wine into his Blood as nourishment for my spiritual life.

Inconvenient Holiness

∞∞∞∞∞∞∞∞∞∞∞∞∞∞∞∞∞∞∞∞∞∞∞∞∞∞∞∞∞

The fruit of the Spirit is . . . patience.
—Galatians 5:22

St. Claude la Columbière (1641–1682) teaches us how to produce the spiritual fruit of patience:

> All our life is sown with tiny thorns that produce in our hearts a thousand involuntary movements of hatred, envy, fear, impatience, a thousand disturbances that momentarily alter our peace of soul. For example, we say something that we shouldn't have said. Or someone says something that hurts our feelings. A child inconveniences you. A bore stops you. You don't like the weather. Your work is not going according to plan. A piece of furniture is broken. A dress is torn. I know that these are not occasions for producing very heroic virtue. But they would definitely be enough to acquire it if we really wished to.[10]

When big things go wrong, the Holy Spirit seems to get me to handle them calmly. But when I am faced with the myriad daily inconveniences of life, I bristle with irritability. If you're like me, you need the grace of the Spirit to transform little nuisances into occasions for growth in holiness.

With G. K. Chesterton, may you regard every inconvenience as "an adventure wrongly considered." May the Holy Spirit, who is tenderhearted and slow to anger, help you replace irritability with patience.

Come, Holy Spirit. Give me the grace to respond to daily disturbances with patience. May every little inconvenience become an occasion for me to grow in holiness.

Help on the Way

<><><><><><><><><><><><><><><><><>

The Spirit said to Philip, "Go and join up
with that chariot."
—Acts 8:29

The Holy Spirit sent Philip to join an Ethiopian
eunuch, a court official returning home from Jerusalem. As he entered the chariot, he noticed that the official was reading verses in Isaiah that described Jesus as
the Lamb of God. When Philip asked him if he understood what he was reading, the Ethiopian said, "How
can I, unless someone instructs me?" (Acts 8:31).
So Philip interpreted the Scripture passage and pro-
claimed Jesus to him. The eunuch was converted on
the spot, stopped the chariot near water, and was baptized. Then the Spirit "snatched Philip away" (8:39),
and the Ethiopian continued on his way rejoicing.

The story of Philip and the Ethiopian has two mes-
sages for you. First, the Spirit may prompt you to

relate to someone that you may be especially gifted to help. Second, like the Ethiopian eunuch, you may need someone to help you understand a Scripture passage. This person could be a priest or teacher in your parish. But often it may be the Holy Spirit, who will teach you if you ask him.

May you learn to recognize the Spirit's invitation to pay attention to the needs of others, and may the Author of the Bible guide you as you seek to understand it and apply its teaching to your life.

O Holy Spirit, I open myself to you. If you will, lead me to people that I can serve in some way. Illumine my mind with your light and wisdom so that I can grasp what you are saying to me in Scripture.

Ladies' Night

The spirit of the LORD shall rest upon him: /
a spirit of . . . [piety].[11]
—Isaiah 11:2

Once I was a discussion leader at a parish evening of renewal, and five women in their eighties joined my table. The speaker asked us to share about our personal experience of Jesus. I was deeply moved by the way these ladies expressed their love for the Lord. One woman came to tears because the name of Jesus meant so much to her. Another told of coming to know Jesus by touching a crucifix cherished in her family. A third remembered an occasion when she sensed Jesus resting his head against her shoulder! "Well," I joked, "he must have thought you were his grandmother." As I reflect on my time with these great women, I believe they showed me what the Spirit's gift of piety is really like. It is a gift that leads us to a profound awareness of God's love for us.

Talking with these holy women challenged me to consider my relationship with Jesus. I hope my writing about them does the same for you. Ask yourself about your piety: How well do you know Jesus? How do you experience him?

May the Holy Spirit rest upon you with a gift of piety so that you may come to know and experience Jesus more and more.

Come, Holy Spirit. Shower your gifts upon me, especially the gift of piety. I want to know Jesus more clearly, love him more dearly, and obey him more nearly.

The Prayer Starter

◇◇◇◇◇◇◇◇◇◇◇◇◇◇◇◇◇◇◇◇◇◇◇◇◇◇◇◇◇◇

God sent the spirit of his Son into our hearts,
crying out, "Abba, Father!"
—Galatians 4:6

You received a spirit of adoption, through which
we cry, "Abba, Father!"
—Romans 8:15

Pope Benedict XVI explains the Holy Spirit's role in
our prayer:

The Holy Spirit is the precious and necessary gift
that makes us children of God. . . . St. Paul's two
passages on this action of the Holy Spirit . . . cor-
respond with each other but contain a different
nuance. [In Galatians] the Apostle says that the
Spirit cries, "Abba! Father!" in us. [In Romans]
he says that it is we who cry, "Abba! Father!" . . .
St. Paul wants to make us understand that

Christian prayer . . . never happens in one direction from us to God, it is never merely "an action of ours," but, rather, is the expression of a reciprocal relationship in which God is the first to act; it is the Holy Spirit who cries in us, and we are able to cry because the impetus comes from the Holy Spirit. . . . [The Holy Spirit] is the prime initiator of prayer so that we may really converse with God and say "Abba" to God.[12]

We tend to think that prayer is something that we do, something that we have to start. But the Holy Spirit is the "prayer starter." He is speaking to us continuously, waiting for us to pray in response.

May you become ever more aware of the Spirit's nearness and ever more alert to his constant efforts to communicate with you.

Come, Holy Spirit. I open my mind and heart to you. I want to hear your divine voice and listen to your words for me, and I want to follow your leadings.

Doing the Wise Thing

*To one is given through the Spirit
the expression of wisdom.*
—*1 Corinthians 12:8*

On a weekend in December 1963, I participated in a Cursillo weekend in South Bend, Indiana. The event was revelatory for me, and I have never been the same since. The gifts of the Holy Spirit were at work in the leaders, especially the "expression of wisdom," which communicates inspired counsel on living the Christian life. For example, one speaker taught about "environments." He explained that we live in a concentric series of social circles: family, relatives, fellow parishioners, friends and neighbors, colleagues, and so on. He persuaded me that I should be praying for people in these environments and watching for opportunities to lead them to the Lord. So from that time, I have kept a list of people in my circles and have prayed for them daily. I have been able to lead some of them closer to Christ, and I'm still working on many others.

I frequently scan my life looking for moments when the Spirit may be giving me an "expression of wisdom." I urge you to do the same. We all need Spirit-led counsel for living the Christian life more faithfully.

May you always recognize the expression of wisdom operating in the people and events that you encounter, and may you wisely act on these workings of the Holy Spirit.

Come, Holy Spirit. Fill me with all spiritual wisdom and understanding so that I may live in a manner worthy of the Lord. Strengthen me with your gifts so that I may become fruitful in service, persevere in trials, and rejoice in all circumstances (Colossians 1:9-12).

Occasions of Grace

✕✕✕✕✕✕✕✕✕✕✕✕✕✕✕✕✕✕✕✕✕✕✕✕✕✕✕✕✕✕

And no one can say "Jesus is Lord,"
except by the holy Spirit.
—1 Corinthians 12:3

Most of my friends who worship at the 7 a.m.
daily Mass are over seventy years old. So when a
young person joins us, I like to greet him. Recently, I
approached a young man after Mass. I jokingly broke
the ice by asking, "What are you doing here?" He
said, "I'm Joey, and I'm here because I love Jesus."
His sincere response touched me. Then Joey asked if
our parish had a pro-life group. He wanted to pray
the Rosary with them at the local abortion clinic, but
he had missed their scheduled day. The next morn-
ing I saw Joey standing alone at the clinic, praying
his Rosary.

I sense the presence of the Holy Spirit in this young disciple. Meeting Joey was an occasion of grace for me. I

am determined to become his friend. Even though I'm three times his age, he has a lot to teach me.

Have you ever introduced yourself as a person who loves Jesus? I don't think I have, but I am watching for a chance to imitate Joey. Do you see anyone like Joey, young or old, in your community? If you do, become his friend and let the Spirit teach you by his example.

> When the occasion presents itself, may you freely identify yourself as a disciple of Jesus. May you find friends filled with the Spirit who can encourage, inspire, and teach you.

Holy Spirit, confirm me in my decision to know, love, and serve Jesus as his disciple. Give me the confidence to speak openly about my loyalty to him.

Behaving Patiently

<><><><><><><><><><><><><><><><><><><><><><>

Be patient in tribulation.
—*Romans 12:12, RSV*

At the turn of the twentieth century, Servant of God Élisabeth Leseur (1866–1914) decided to dedicate her life fully to Christ. Ironically, what occasioned her spiritual awakening was the attempt of her husband, Felix, to get her to read Renan's atheistic *Life of Jesus*. From that time the Holy Spirit seems to have invaded her soul, advancing her in intimacy with the Lord and giving her the patience to endure the circumstances of her life. Sick for many years with hepatitis, Élisabeth's condition worsened after 1908. In 1911 she was diagnosed with cancer. She calmly accepted the intense pain of the disease and applied it as prayer for her husband. After Élisabeth's death in 1914, Felix discovered in her journal that she had quietly offered years of great suffering for his conversion. He was so moved that he not only embraced

Christ but also became a Dominican priest who traveled throughout Europe speaking about his wife's spiritual writings.

When we endure rough circumstances, we may feel more aggravated than patient. But patience is more of a behavior than a feeling. Patience is what we do with the grace the Spirit gives us to get through difficulties.

When you face challenges of any kind, may you count on the Holy Spirit to lead you through them with patient endurance. May you apply your suffering as prayer for someone facing a greater difficulty than you are.

Holy Spirit, Power divine, / fill and nerve this will of mine; / grant that I may strongly live, / bravely bear, and nobly strive. (from an 1864 hymn by Samuel Longfellow)

Getting Free

<><><><><><><><><><><><><><><>

Bless the LORD, *my soul. . . . / Who redeems your life*
from the pit, / and crowns you
with mercy and compassion.
—*Psalm 103:2, 4*

Fr. Ed, the associate pastor in my parish and my
friend, says he was a drunk for sixteen years of his
priesthood. He tried rehab programs, but his alcohol-
ism always prevailed. Finally, his West Coast bishop
gave up hope and dismissed him from his priestly service. Fr. Ed came to central Florida, where he joined
our parish incognito. Fr. Paul, the pastor, befriended
him and introduced him to an AA sponsor. Improve-
ment was slow and hard, but one afternoon something miraculous happened. While Fr. Ed was relax-
ing in the Florida sunshine, the Holy Spirit struck
and delivered him from his addiction. Restored to his
priestly service by the bishop, he has served us generously for two decades.

We all have habitual behaviors that we'd like to be freed from. Minor faults like persistent irritability may afflict us, or we may be bound up by more serious addictions like those to alcohol, drugs, pornography, or some other compulsion. Like Fr. Ed, who joined AA, we may need professional help. Like him, we should expect the Holy Spirit to intervene and set us free.

> When you find yourself trapped in some compulsive behavior, may your friends embrace you with love and compassion. May you confidently turn to the Holy Spirit, expecting him to set you free.

O Holy Spirit, I sometimes feel as though I am trapped in a pit. I look to you with faith and ask you to lift me up and set me free.

The Humble Healer

◇◇◇◇◇◇◇◇◇◇◇◇◇◇◇◇◇◇◇◇◇◇◇◇◇◇◇◇◇◇

To one is given . . . gifts of healing by the one Spirit.
—1 Corinthians 12:8, 9

In 1603 St. Martin de Porres (1579–1639) became a brother in the Dominican monastery at Lima, Peru. From his youth, Martin was trained as a physician, but he also possessed supernatural gifts of healing. To keep himself humble, he always attempted to conceal his healing gift by using some herb or poultice as a decoy when he ministered to the sick.

For example, once Martin prayed for a woman whom doctors had diagnosed with a life-threatening hemorrhage. He told her that the Lord had revealed to him that she would recover. Then, to conceal his miraculous powers, he gave her an apple to eat. As he predicted, in a few days she had returned to perfect health. At another time, he prayed for the healing of an ailing archbishop and had no decoys with him. His healing gift plainly exposed, he returned to the monastery, and to humble himself, he swept floors and cleaned toilets.

When we or those close to us are sick or injured, we should seek healing through the sacrament of anointing and the intercession of friends. We should expect a healing—the Lord may grant one, or he may give us something better.

> When you or your loved ones are sick, injured, or distressed by any kind of pain, may you experience healing through the sacraments and through the prayer of friends.

Come, Holy Spirit. Increase my faith so that I may expect you to heal me and my loved ones. Increase my trust in you so that I may always accept your answers to my prayers.

Becoming a Saint

<><><><><><><><><><><><><><><><><><><><><>

I will put my Spirit within you, and you shall live.
—*Ezekiel 37:14, RSV*

St. Thomas Aquinas (ca. 1225–1275) explains how the Holy Spirit makes us holy:

No one is holy unless the Holy Spirit makes him holy. . . . In all whom He makes holy, He renders them . . . contemptuous of temporal things. As it says in John's Gospel: "If anyone loves the world, the love of the Father is not in him" (1 John 2:15). Again, He bestows spiritual life upon those whom He makes holy, as it says in Ezekiel: "Behold I will place the spirit within you, and you shall live" (37:5). The spiritual life owes its very existence to the Holy Spirit. "If you live by the Spirit, walk also by the Spirit" (Galatians 5:25). . . . Again, the Holy Spirit leads them back to the hidden origin through which we are united to God; in the words of Isaiah, "the Spirit of the Lord will carry you away to a place you do not know" (1 Kings 18:12), that is, to the heavenly inheritance.[13]

The Second Vatican Council called us to holiness, inviting us to dispose ourselves to become saints through prayer and a life of discipleship. But nothing we do can make us holy. That's the exclusive work of the Spirit, who makes us saints if we ask him to.

May you open your heart wide to welcome the Holy Spirit and his graces. May you cooperate with the Spirit's desire to make you holy by deciding that you want to become a saint.

O Holy Spirit, I renounce any attachments that block my openness to you. I give my life to you and want you to make me holy.

Spirit-Led Service

<><><><><><><><><><><><><><><><><><>

To each is given the manifestation of the Spirit
for the common good.
—1 Corinthians 12:7, RSV

My friend Deacon Henry Libersat preaches with great effect. He is well prepared for his service. Henry has read widely in Catholic theology for the past five decades, and he has immersed himself in Scripture during his training for the deaconate and in his leadership of our parish men's Bible study. When Henry is scheduled to preach, he spends weeks researching the text he has chosen, talking about it with friends, and meditating on it. All this preparation creates the opportunity for the Holy Spirit to act when he speaks. The Spirit picks up Henry's thoughts and charges them with life-changing energy. Henry says he can tell when the Holy Spirit engages him—he senses the Spirit's presence, is filled with peace, feels certainty about his message, and receives words he had not planned to use. In this way, the Spirit makes Henry himself a gift to our parish community.

Every Christian (and that means you and me) has received spiritual gifts for service. Over the years I have discovered my gifts for writing, teaching, and encouraging. What gifts has he given you? Are you using them for "the common good"?

> May the Holy Spirit show you your spiritual gifts and guide you in using them well, and may he give you as a gift to your community.

O Holy Spirit, I want to work along with you to build up the Christian community. So I open myself to discover and accept the gifts you want to give me for service in the Church.

An Open Heart

◇◇◇◇◇◇◇◇◇◇◇◇◇◇◇◇◇◇◇◇◇

May [the Father], through his Spirit, enable you to grow firm in power with regard to your inner self.
—*Ephesians 3:16, NJB*

St. Lutgarde (1182–1246) was a beautiful, worldly young woman. Her parents had placed her under the care of Benedictines at a monastery, who allowed her some freedoms. She was even able to entertain young men in the garden. But one day Jesus appeared to Lutgarde, and she gave her heart to him. She immediately began to devote herself to the Lord in prayer, and he favored her with an intimate sense of his presence. Once, for example, while meditating after Mass, Lutgarde asked the Lord to go heal her friend Sr. Elizabeth while Lutgarde took a break and went for a snack. And that's what happened—Lutgarde got her meal and the Lord healed Elizabeth! The saint spent four decades at the monastery, dedicating herself to adoration before the Blessed Sacrament and intercession.

St. Lutgarde's example tells us that no matter what we are like or where we are in our lives, God is after us. He chases us down to draw us to himself. All we need to do is imitate Lutgarde, open our hearts to him, and spend time with him in prayer.

May you have a keen eye and sensitive ear for the Lord's approaches and invitations. Like St. Lutgarde, may you give him your heart so that you may come to experience an intimate sense of his presence.

Holy Spirit, . . . / Enter each aspiring heart, / occupy its inmost part / with your dazzling purity. / All that gives to us our worth, / all that benefits the earth, / you bring to maturity. (Veni Sancte Spiritus)

A Little Miracle

*There are varieties of working, but it is
the same God who inspires them all
in every one. . . . To one is given through
the Spirit . . . the working of miracles.*
—1 Corinthians 12:6, 8, 10, RSV

One week after my wife, Mary Lou, was hired at the
local public library, she misplaced the keys to the
building. We prayed fervently and searched every-
where but could not find the key. On the morn-
ing that Mary Lou had decided to report the loss, I
prayed, "Lord, let me find that key now." Then I felt
led to search Mary Lou's van. Since we had searched
it many times before, I was not hopeful, but when I
looked under the driver's seat, the key was right there
in plain sight!

How had that happened? Had we simply not seen it
before? Had some child played a silly prank, wised

up, and then put it where we would find it? Or did the Lord put it there because he loves Mary Lou? No matter. We just thanked him for a little miracle.

The Holy Spirit is not a vending machine, dispensing miracles at our request. But when you face hard circumstances, don't hesitate to pray, and then expect him to act. He may give you what you ask for, or he may give you something better.

> When bad things happen and you seem to face imponderable challenges, may you have the confidence to ask the Holy Spirit to give you a little breakthrough miracle.

Come, Holy Spirit. Give me the spiritual spine I need to act in faith. Increase my confidence in you so that I can approach you with expectation.

The Holy Spirit and Us

<><><><><><><><><><><><><><><><><><><><><><><><><><>

It is the decision of the holy Spirit and of us
not to place on you any burden.
—Acts 15:28

Around AD 50, the apostles held a council in Jerusalem, which is regarded as a prototype of the subsequent twenty-one ecumenical councils of the Catholic Church. The council decided that gentile converts were not obligated to keep most of the Mosaic law. Significantly, the letter reported that the council's decision came from the cooperation of the Holy Spirit with the leaders. From Nicea in 325 to Vatican II in 1962, the Holy Spirit has collaborated with the popes and bishops to steer the Church through many challenges that required defending the faith and reforming practices. This should make us confident that the Holy Spirit will guide the Church through any circumstances that may come, no matter how dire.

Not only does the Spirit collaborate with popes and bishops, but he also works with pastors and laypersons in parishes. We should be praying to the Holy Spirit daily for the whole Church and for our parish communities.

May the Spirit give you wisdom about the ways in which he works among us in the Church, inspiring you with confidence in our leaders and guiding you in your Christian service.

Come, Holy Spirit, fill the hearts of your faithful and enkindle in them the fire of your love. Send forth your Spirit and they shall be created. And you shall renew the face of the earth.

No Mere Mortals

Be transformed by the renewal of your mind, that
you may discern what is the will of God.
—Romans 12:2

Late one evening many years ago, I experienced a life-changing revelation while reading C. S. Lewis's essay "The Weight of Glory." These words struck me and made me look at people in a new way: "There are no *ordinary* people. You have never talked to a mere mortal. Nations, cultures, arts, civilizations—these are mortal, and their life is to ours as the life of a gnat. But it is immortals whom we joke with, work with, marry, snub, and exploit—immortal horrors or everlasting splendors."[14] All day long, Lewis said, with everything we say and do, we are moving people toward one of these two destinations. As I put down the book, I felt as though the Holy Spirit were stripping scales from my eyes. Since that night five decades ago, I have treated my wife, children, relatives, friends, neighbors—in fact, everyone I know and meet—with a renewed vision and awe.

Every day you have opportunities to move many people closer to their eternal destiny. If you realize that they are immortals, you will watch what you say and do. By following Jesus' command to love others as he has loved us, you will be helping them on their way to becoming "everlasting splendors."

> May you stay alert for the revelations of the Spirit. May scales fall from your eyes so that you may see everyone and everything with awe.

Come, Holy Spirit. Sharpen my ability to notice your leadings, and touch my will with the grace to do what you want me to do.

Strengthened for Suffering

~~~~~~

But you will receive power when the holy Spirit
comes upon you, and you will be my witnesses.
—Acts 1:8

Scripture scholar Fr. George Montague, SM, explains
how the Spirit helps us through suffering:

Felicity was one of two women thrown to the
beasts in the Roman arena. She was pregnant
and gave birth to her child while in prison. The
guard mocked her in her birthing pains, saying
that it would be a lot worse when the beasts
attacked her in the arena. Felicity replied, "My
sufferings here are mine. But there another will
be suffering with me." Every age of the Church
has had its martyrs. . . . Jesus said that the Holy
Spirit would empower his disciples to be witnesses (the original meaning of "martyr"). If,
then, the Holy Spirit is the power that enables

Christians to follow Jesus to a martyr's death, what power he must give us to carry our daily crosses![15]

Likely, none of us will die as martyrs, but all of us will face suffering. Jesus said that we would pay the cost of discipleship by taking up our cross daily and following him (Luke 9:23). But he also promised that the Holy Spirit would strengthen us to endure whatever comes.

May you count on the Holy Spirit to empower you to carry your crosses. May you sense the Lord's presence when you are suffering sickness, loss, failure, or some other cause of pain.

I entrust everything to you, O Holy Spirit, and I am comforted to know that you are with me when I am suffering. You are my strength, my support, and my safety.

Making Peace

◇◇◇◇◇◇◇◇◇◇◇◇◇◇◇◇◇◇◇

The fruit of the Spirit is . . . peace.
—Galatians 5:22

From his days in the seminary to his death, Angelo Roncalli, the future Pope St. John XXIII (1881–1963), treated every person he met with respect and built peaceful relationships with them. When he became a bishop in 1925, he took as his motto "Obedience and Peace," and this oriented his life. Popes sent Roncalli as their representative to Bulgaria, Turkey, and Greece, where he befriended leaders of the Orthodox Church, whom he later invited to attend the Second Vatican Council. As pope, he saw himself as being divinely commissioned to build bridges with all people of goodwill, even Communists and atheists. He intended that the council be a witness toward achieving the Lord's prayer that all may be one (John 17:21). Just before he died, he published his encyclical *Pacem in Terris* (Peace on Earth), which summed up his vision and practice.

Pope St. John XXIII's example shows us that peace, while it may include good feelings, is mainly behavior that maintains unity in relationships. We must take stock of how we relate to others and imitate this pope by treating everyone with respect and friendliness.

May you treat everyone, even people you do not like, with friendly respect. May you be known as a woman or man of peace.

I open my heart to you, O Holy Spirit. Give me the grace to realize how I must change to make peace the binding force in all my relationships.

Healing Graces

◇◇◇◇◇◇◇◇◇◇◇◇◇◇◇◇◇◇◇◇◇◇◇

Jesus went around to all the towns and villages, . . .
curing every disease and illness.
—Matthew 9:35

Jesus arranged for the Holy Spirit to continue his healing ministry in the Church. Over many years, my wife and I have experienced the Spirit's healing graces in our family. When a child became ill, we prayed for them and then got medical help. Our kids seemed to recover more quickly than expected, which I believe was the Spirit's doing. We remember one healing that resembles a miracle. One afternoon our six-year-old daughter screamed as she fell from a swing. We ran from the house to aid her but saw that our two-year-old son was drinking from a can of charcoal lighter fluid. We prayed over the child while we rushed him to the emergency room. To our great relief, the medical staff determined that he had not been poisoned. The Spirit had the whole event in his care, even letting our daughter's cry signal to us that our son was in danger.

Before someone in your family gets injured or ill, you should entrust them to God in daily prayer. Then when something happens to them, you can approach the Lord with expectant faith and ask him for healing.

> May you come to love the Lord so much that you trust him without question. When you ask him for healing, may you receive his answer with joy and confidence. May you realize that he may give you something better than what you have requested.

O Lord, I place all my trust in you. Send me the Holy Spirit to increase my faith so that I can pray for healing with confidence and receive with joy whatever graces he may send.

The Water of Life

For in one Spirit we were all baptized into one body,
whether Jews or Greeks, slaves or free persons, and
we were all given to drink of one Spirit.
—1 Corinthians 12:13

St. Irenaeus (ca. 130–200) teaches how the Holy
Spirit makes us one in Christ:

> This was why the Lord had promised to send
> the Advocate: he was to prepare us as an offer-
> ing to God. Like dry flour, which cannot become
> one lump of dough, one loaf of bread, without
> moisture, we who are many could not become
> one in Christ Jesus without the water that comes
> down from heaven. And like parched ground,
> which yields no harvest unless it receives mois-
> ture, we who were once like a waterless tree
> could never have lived and borne fruit with-
> out this abundant rainfall from above. Through

the baptism that liberates us from change and decay, we have become one in body; through the Spirit we have become one in soul.[16]

The Holy Spirit himself is the water of life that incorporates us into the body of Christ. We should regularly pray for the renewal of our baptism, and we should let the Holy Spirit flow through us, cleansing us and joining us to one another.

May you expect the Holy Spirit to refresh your baptismal graces, and may you experience the fullness of life in the Spirit in the body of Christ.

Holy Spirit, . . . With your soft refreshing rains, / break our drought, remove our stains; / bind up all our injuries. / Grant enabling energy, / courage in adversity, / joys that last forevermore. (Veni Sancte Spiritus)

The Teacher of Everything

*The Paraclete, the Holy Spirit, whom the Father
will send in my name, will teach you everything and
remind you of all I have said to you.*
—John 14:26, NJB

When I was a sophomore in college, I participated in
a Bible study on the Gospel of John. I had never studied Scripture before, so I often felt lost in the conversation. But when we came upon this verse, I believe
that the Holy Spirit struck me with awe: "Anyone
who loves me will keep my word, and my Father
will love him, and we shall come to him and make a
home in him" (John 14:23, NJB). My heart leapt at
the thought! God the Father loved *me,* and he and
Jesus had taken up residence in me. From that time
five decades ago, that verse has oriented my life. It
comes to mind often, and it thrills me to realize that
the eternal, unchangeable, infinite, almighty, and all
loving God dwells in me.

When we read Scripture, we should expect the Holy Spirit to open its meaning for us and to "teach [us] everything." What better teacher about the Bible could we have than the Author himself?

When you read Scripture, may the Holy Spirit enlighten you and open you to its meaning for your life. May he lead you to passages that strike you with awe and enliven your faith.

O God, who by the light of the Holy Spirit did instruct the hearts of the faithful, grant that by the same Holy Spirit we may be truly wise and ever enjoy his consolations, through Christ our Lord. Amen.

An Excess of Compassion

*Put on then, as God's chosen ones,
holy and beloved, heartfelt compassion.*
—Colossians 3:12

Paul Scott was a victim of leprosy, and it left him badly disfigured. Once he approached Bishop Fulton J. Sheen for help, and the bishop responded to him with an excess of compassion. He helped Paul find and furnish an apartment, bought him food and clothing, and encouraged him to take a job behind the scenes in a social agency. The bishop hosted the young man for dinner once a week and helped him cut his food. When Sheen was installed as archbishop of Rochester, he invited Paul to sit in the cathedral as an honored guest. I think St. Paul would want us to regard such exemplary compassion as a fruit of the Spirit, even though he did not include it in his list in Galatians (5:22-23).

Every day you bump into people whose circumstances appeal to you for compassion. Be ready to encourage the single mom with an unruly toddler, help an elderly man carry his groceries to the car, or meet some need for a troubled friend. St. Paul says to "put on compassion" so that you respond to others with Spirit-led concern.

May you have the eyes to notice the needs of others and the heart to respond to them with compassion.

O Holy Spirit, I open my heart to you. Come to me and help me open my heart with genuine concern for others.

Mary Opens Us to the Spirit

<><><><><><><><><><><><><><><><><><><><><><><><><><><><><>

When the time for Pentecost was fulfilled, they were all in one place together.
—*Acts 2:1*

Scripture scholar Fr. George Montague explains Mary's role at Pentecost:

> Having experienced her Pentecost at the annunciation, Mary was doubtless the one who inspired this first intercessory prayer of the gathered Church. Paul would later say that the Holy Spirit intercedes within the Christian "with inexpressible groanings" (Romans 8:26). Inasmuch as the rest of the community had not yet received this outpouring of the Spirit, they must have looked to Mary to show them how to pray in the Spirit in this way. The gift of the Holy Spirit would be new for the disciples. For Mary it would bring a deeper union with her Spouse. . . . These days of preparation for Pentecost contain an important

lesson. Our ability to receive the Holy Spirit is in proportion to our intense desire and preparation for him. How big a container will we bring to this "Niagara Falls"? A thimble or a barrel? He will always overflow whatever container we bring. . . . But we choose the size of the container.[17]

When we pray for a renewal of the Spirit, we should ask Mary to intercede for us as she did at Pentecost. We should prepare our hearts for the Spirit by imitating her openness.

May Mary's intercession open you to receiving a fresh release of the Holy Spirit, and may she help you accept his gifts.

Hail Mary, full of grace, the Lord is with you. Blessed are you among women, and blessed is the fruit of your womb, Jesus. Mary, intercede with your Son for a new outpouring of the Spirit on me. Help me be open to receiving his gifts.

Words of Encouragement

<><><><><><><><><><><><><><><><><><><><><><><><><>

Encourage one another and build
one another up, as indeed you do.
—*1 Thessalonians 5:11*

About twenty years ago, I attended the "On-Pur-pose Person Seminar." Its promise was that after three days, participants would be able to understand the theme that oriented their lives. At the end of the process, I arrived at three words that "defined" me: an "encourager with words." I comfortably agreed with that characterization because I believe that the Holy Spirit moves me to encourage others through my writing, teaching, and one-on-one conversations. I regard my spoken encouragement as a spiritual gift. I do so because building up others—at home, at a parish meeting, in my neighborhood, at the gro-cery store, and so on—flows from me without fore-thought. I believe that I am inspired to communicate something of God's love and approval to the people

I encounter. As for my encouragement through writing and teaching, judge for yourself as you read this book.

When people encourage you, accept their words and let them soak into your heart. Never brush off praise for an accomplishment by saying, "It was all God, not me." That attitude may be disregarding God's way of expressing love and approval for you through a friend.

> When someone praises you during the day,
> may you breathe it in, and may you take time
> at night to breathe it out in thanks and praise
> to God.

O Holy Spirit, you have adopted me as a child in the divine family. I come before you strengthened by your encouragement, and I give you thanks and praise for all that you do for me.

Spiritual Equilibrium

✧✧✧✧✧✧✧✧✧✧✧✧✧✧✧✧✧✧✧✧✧✧✧✧✧✧✧✧✧✧✧✧

He will baptize you with the holy Spirit and fire.
—Luke 3:16

St. Teresa of Avila (1515–1582) claims that she was a "gadabout" nun for twenty years, not getting serious about her spirituality until she was forty. Then a series of extraordinary encounters with Christ launched her spiritual growth. Once while she was praying the *Veni Creator Spiritus,* she seemed to hear the Lord say, "I will not have you hold conversations with men but with angels." From that time, St. Teresa enjoyed frequent heaven-sent experiences of God's presence. Her closeness to the Lord spurred her to spend herself in service. From 1560 until her death in 1582, she founded seventeen renewed Carmelite convents in Spain. She also spearheaded a general renewal of Catholic life, leading many into a deeper relationship with Christ that continues to this day through her spiritual classics on prayer.

St. Teresa models the balanced Catholic life, praying as if everything depended on God and serving as if everything depended on her. I think most of us get a little out of balance. We tend to spend ourselves in service and neglect our prayer life. Praying the *Veni Creator Spiritus* can help us restore our spiritual equilibrium.

May the Holy Spirit breathe new life into you
and set your heart on fire for loving the Lord
in prayer and serving him in others.

Come, Creator Spirit, come. / . . . You who are called the Paraclete, / best gift of God above, / the living spring, the vital fire, / sweet christ'ning and true love. (Veni Creator Spiritus)

Reality Checks

◇◇◇◇◇◇◇◇◇◇◇◇◇◇◇◇◇◇◇◇

In those days [Jesus] departed to the mountain to
pray, and he spent the night in prayer to God.
—Luke 6:12

Let me be clear—I have never prayed all night. But at transition points in my life, I have spent hours seeking direction from the Holy Spirit. For example, four times when I needed to change jobs, I took long prayer times asking for his guidance. Each time he led me to a new and better opportunity. I have also made it a regular practice to take a couple of hours for a prayerful reality check. I take my Bible to a park, pray my favorite psalms, and then ask the Lord if I'm doing what he wants me to do. I review my life, my care for my family, my service in the Church and at work. I spend quiet time listening to the Spirit and note any leadings that either affirm or correct my course. Then I look for ways of doing what I'm told.

If you are at a transition point, I encourage you to spend time seeking the Holy Spirit's guidance. If you are in a secure place, I recommend that you take prayerful reality checks throughout the year.

> May you find silence amid the daily noise
> where you can hear the voice of the Spirit,
> and may you have the wisdom and fortitude
> to do what he tells you.

Come, Holy Spirit. I open my mind and heart to you. I want you to guide me so that I can lead a life pleasing to you, one that brings love and blessing to others.

Speaking from Experience

◇◇

*I want to learn only this from you: did you receive
the Spirit from works of the law, or from
faith in what you heard?*
—Galatians 3:2

St. Paul wrote an angry letter to the Galatians
because they were embracing legalism instead of
Christian freedom. He challenged them, expecting
them to answer him from their experience of the
Holy Spirit: "Did you experience so many things in
vain? . . . Does, then, the one who supplies the Spirit
to you and works mighty deeds among you do so
from works of the law or from faith in what you
heard?" (3:4, 5). I find his argument both intriguing
and inspiring. Intriguing, because Paul expected his
readers to readily recognize their personal experience
of the Holy Spirit. Inspiring, because Paul's questions
make me want to experience the Holy Spirit as fully
as the Galatians did.

We have received the Holy Spirit in the sacraments. But if St. Paul were to ask us questions that he expected us to answer from our experience of the Spirit, I suspect we might be puzzled and speechless. If we have let the Holy Spirit lie dormant in our lives, we must stir him up and count on him to act.

May you respond to the Lord's promise of the Holy Spirit with faith and expect him to work in you so that you will readily experience him and his gifts.

O Holy Spirit, I know that you are with me and in me. I ask with confidence that you let me experience your presence and power. Like the Galatians, I want to be able to see the evidence of your action in my life.

The Spirit Is In You

><><><><><><><><><><><><><><><><><><><><><><><><

If by the Spirit you put to death the habits
originating in the body, you will have life.
—Romans 8:13, NJB

St. Paul explains how the Holy Spirit enables us to conquer our evil inclinations:

Those who live by their natural inclinations can never be pleasing to God. You, however, live not by your natural inclinations, but by the Spirit, since the Spirit of God has made a home in you. . . . And if the Spirit of him who raised Jesus from the dead has made his home in you, then he who raised Christ Jesus from the dead will give life to your own mortal bodies through his Spirit living in you. . . . We have no obligation to human nature to be dominated by it. If you do live in that way, you are doomed to die; but if by the Spirit you put to death the habits originating in the body, you will have life. (Romans 8:8-9, 11-13, NJB)

This is very good news. We all struggle with strong temptations and besetting sins, but the Holy Spirit has made his home in us. We can engage his power to say no to the evil inclinations that come from our flawed human nature.

May you welcome the Holy Spirit who dwells within you. May you invite him to help you put to death your evil inclinations by saying no to them and replacing them with good behaviors.

O Holy Spirit, you know me through and through. You see how I struggle with temptations and how often I fall into sin. Please strengthen me to say no to my bad inclinations, and give me the grace to behave uprightly.

Inspired Repartee

<><><><><><><><><><><><><><><><><><><><>

It will not be you who speak but the Spirit of your
Father speaking through you.
—Matthew 10:20

St. Polycarp (d. 155), a disciple of St. John, served
as bishop of Smyrna for five decades. During a sec-
ond-century persecution, a mob demanded that
he deny Christ or be fed to the wild animals in the
arena. When his pursuers came to arrest him, Polycarp served them a meal, and while they were eating,
he prayed. Then he was taken to the arena, where
the governor ordered Polycarp to deny Christ and
denounce Christians by saying, "Away with the atheists!" Polycarp looked at the mob of pagans in the
arena and shaking his fist at them, he looked up to
heaven and said, "Away with these atheists!"

Only the Holy Spirit could have staged such a dra-
matic repartee. Realizing that Polycarp was unafraid

of the wild beasts, the governor attempted to burn Polycarp at the stake. Miraculously, the fire did not consume him, so he was killed with a dagger. The account of Polycarp's martyrdom has encouraged Christians for centuries.

Our thoroughly secularized culture will surely give you chances to profess your loyalty to Jesus or defend your faith. When such occasions present themselves, you can count on the Holy Spirit to give you the right words to say.

When someone mocks you or challenges your faith, may you speak with positive conviction and with words prompted by the Holy Spirit.

O Holy Spirit, give me the fortitude to defend the faith and the wisdom to follow your leadings and to speak with respect, patience, and kindness.

Divine Mysteries

◇◇◇◇◇◇◇◇◇◇◇◇◇◇◇◇◇◇◇◇◇◇◇◇◇◇

Send out your light and your truth;
they shall be my guide.
—Psalm 43:3, NJB

My hobby is reading mystery novels. Strange as it may seem, I find spiritual wisdom in these books. The ancient Jews prayed for "light and truth" to guide them through dangers on the way to Jerusalem. And I see in the best mysteries "light and truth," which guide me on my way through the dangers of our sin-bent world.

Among my favorites are the stories of twentieth-century author Rex Stout. His main characters, Nero Wolfe and Archie Goodwin, live in a brownstone in New York. Wolfe has made his home a place of safety and uprightness, where all evil is unwelcome. He uses his extraordinary brainpower to bring criminals to justice. Archie, his streetwise associate, assists him.

Rex Stout's stories draw me into Wolfe's safe haven and make me appreciate the safety and uprightness I find in the Lord's house.

We need to let the Holy Spirit point us to the good elements in our culture. We must learn to observe the ways in which he may be working in our world and listen for his voice in places we might never expect to hear him.

When you find yourself in social environments that are bent away from the Lord, may the Spirit's light and truth guide you through all danger to safety and uprightness.

Come, Holy Spirit. May your kindness and faithful love pursue me every day of my life, and may I make my home in your house of safety and uprightness forever (see Psalm 23:6).

A Generous Spirit

❖❖❖❖❖❖❖❖❖❖❖❖❖❖❖❖❖❖❖❖❖❖❖

The fruit of the Spirit is . . . generosity.
—Galatians 5:22

St. Fabiola (d. 399), a highborn woman of Rome, divorced her abusive and unfaithful husband. But she remarried before he died, in violation of Church law, and was excommunicated. When her second husband died, she repented, performed public penance, and was restored to communion with the Church. As a sign of her repentance, and with the inspiration of the Spirit, Fabiola sold her extensive properties and possessions and gave the money to the poor. Then she established the first public hospital in the Western world, where she personally cared for dying patients.

You may not have done anything as seriously wrong as Fabiola, but you may imitate her generous example. To show repentance for some sin, you might give a favorite article of clothing, a cherished vase or book, or some other valuable item to a poor neighbor.

May you respond to the Spirit by giving freely of your substance to people in need, and may the grace of the giving loop back to you, forming in you the fruit of generosity.

Come, Holy Spirit. Loosen my grip on my "stuff." Give me the grace of generosity and a greater freedom to share myself or my possessions with the poor.

Praying in Tongues

<><><><><><><><><><><><><><><><><><><><>

*And they were all filled with the holy Spirit and
begin to speak in different tongues, as the Spirit
enabled them to proclaim.*
—*Acts 2:4*

Scripture scholar Fr. George Montague, SM, reflects
on praying in tongues:

The fire of the Holy Spirit at Pentecost turned
the huddled community of the disciples into a
blaze of praise. This praise did not consist in
just reciting prayers or psalms of praise. It was
so powerful that it broke the verbal barrier and
gushed forth in tongues. That was the first sign
that the Holy Spirit had truly come upon the
community. So it is meant to be for us when we
receive the Holy Spirit. . . . We are moved to
give our lips and our tongue over to the Holy
Spirit so that his praise can flow through us. . . .

Yielding to tongues may look and feel like going back to infancy. In fact, it is just the opposite. It is not going back before reason; it is going beyond it. . . . It is the heart talking to God beyond the limits of ordinary speech. St. Augustine called it a "jubilation."[18]

Praying in tongues is a gift available to anyone who has received the Holy Spirit. Many of the 120 million Catholics who participate in the Catholic Charismatic Renewal pray in tongues. They say this prayer gift opens them to experience the prayer of adoration.

May the Holy Spirit give you the gift of praise,
and of praying in tongues if you desire it.

Lord Jesus, renew me in the Holy Spirit, and give me the spiritual gifts I need for praise and service. (If you desire the gift of praying in tongues, ask the Lord for it.)

Encouraging Words

〰〰〰〰〰〰〰〰〰〰〰〰〰〰〰〰〰

*There are different workings but the same God who
produces all of them in everyone. . . . To one is given
through the Spirit . . . prophecy.*
—*1 Corinthians 12:6, 8, 10*

In 1403 St. Bernardine of Siena (1380–1444) joined
the Franciscans. For twelve years he lived quietly in
Fiesole, Italy. But in 1417, a novice prophesied to
him three times. "Brother Bernardine," he exclaimed,
"stop hiding your gifts. Go to Lombardy, where all
await you!" The saint went obediently to Milan, not
knowing what to do. But when his eloquence began
to draw huge congregations, he soon discovered that
his vocation was preaching.

Thousands came to hear this entertaining friar, who
used his humor and wisdom to penetrate their souls
with truth. For a quarter century, Bernardine criss-
crossed Italy on foot, calling people to repentance

and holiness. The novice who used a spiritual gift of prophecy planted a seed in the saint that produced a great harvest.

You probably don't think of yourself as a prophet. But the Holy Spirit can work in you to speak prophetically to another. So look for chances to encourage a person to use her obvious gifts to serve the Lord and the Church. You may plant a seed that will produce a great harvest.

> May you always appreciate the gifts of others and encourage them to use such gifts in the service of Christ and the gospel.

O Holy Spirit, teach me to recognize and appreciate the gifts of my relatives and friends. Give me the words to encourage them to exercise their gifts for you and the Church.

Another Advocate

*I will ask the Father, and he will give you another
Advocate to be with you always.*
—John 14:16

In the ancient Greek legal system, an advocate spoke
on behalf of another in court. The term came to be
associated with many other meanings, including
"spokesman," "intercessor," "mediator," "counselor,"
"comforter," and "consoler." Jesus, our first Advocate, is all of these and more. Most of all, he is our
supreme intercessor with the Father, who gave himself as a ransom for our sins and those of the whole
world (1 John 2:2). So that he would not leave us
orphans (John 14:18), Jesus gave us the Holy Spirit
as another Advocate, who would be our teacher and
a witness to him. So the Spirit stays with us to defend,
counsel, and console us and to speak and intercede
for us.

Every day we need a defender against all the challenges to which our culture subjects us. Issues pop up that demand the aid of a counselor. We suffer physical and emotional pain, which makes us long for an intercessor and consoler. How good it is that Jesus has sent us another Advocate to remain with us and surround us with graces.

> From sunrise to sunset, throughout the evening and into the night, whether you are awake or asleep, may you be aware of the companionship of your Advocate, the Holy Spirit.

O Holy Spirit, I rejoice that you stand with me as my Advocate. Come, teach me your ways, counsel me with your wisdom, defend me from temptations to sin, and intercede for me, for I stand in need of your grace.

Gifted to Serve

<><><><><><><><><><><><><><><>

*To each is given the manifestation of the
Spirit for the common good.*
—*1 Corinthians 12:7, RSV*

St. Francis Xavier (1506–1552) was wealthy, well educated, and headed for a career as a professor of theology. But he linked up with St. Ignatius of Loyola (1491–1556) and became one of the first Jesuits. When Ignatius decided to send him as an evangelist to India, Xavier worried that he was not gifted for that service. But on the ship to the East, by example and word, this elegant aristocrat introduced rough seamen to Christ. Within a decade, from India to Japan, he evangelized and baptized thousands. What happened that made him so effective? The Holy Spirit gave him the gifts he needed to bring to Christ and the Church the people he was called to serve.

The Lord may be calling you to perform a service that you do not feel gifted to accomplish. But if God wants you to do some work—for example, to reach out to someone in your neighborhood or lead a group or ministry in your parish—you can count on the Holy Spirit to equip you.

May you embrace whatever service you are called to do, and may you be open to receiving from the Spirit the gifts you need to accomplish it.

Come, Holy Spirit. Show me what I must do to serve Jesus as his disciple. With all my heart, I want to do whatever he wants me to do to advance his work. I don't always feel that I am equipped to serve him, but I expect you to give me the gifts that I need, as you did for St. Francis Xavier.

The Spirit's Priorities

Speak, LORD, for your servant is listening.
—1 Samuel 3:9

In 1975 I was working full-time and devoting myself to writing my first book. One evening in prayer, I heard the Holy Spirit warning me that I was neglecting my family. "Your book will last ten years," he said, "but your family will last forever." Well, he caught my attention! I made some big changes—such as spending regular time with each child, gathering the family every night for sharing before bedtime, and having a weekly family night. In 1985, exactly ten years after the book was published, I received a letter from my publisher informing me that it was going out of print.

Have you thought recently about your priorities? The Holy Spirit wants you to devote your time to the most important areas of your life. So spend some quiet time and listen for his direction.

When urgent matters press on you or when you find yourself engulfed in petty matters, may you listen carefully and discern the guidance of the Holy Spirit.

Speak to me, Lord, for I am listening. Show me how you want me to be spending my time. I want my priorities to align with your priorities for me.

Getting Self under Control

The fruit of the Spirit is . . . self-control.
—Galatians 5:22-23

In his *Confessions,* St. Augustine (354–430) describes himself as a self-indulgent sinner. From his youth he was captivated by the excitement of sex. He lived with a concubine for fifteen years and had a son by her. After meeting St. Ambrose in Milan, Augustine experienced a gradual conversion, and by 386, all that remained was his sexual addiction. "Make me chaste," he would pray, "but not yet."

Then one day when Augustine was struggling to get free of his besetting sin, the Holy Spirit intervened. Augustine heard a child's voice chanting repeatedly, "Take and read!" Recognizing the voice as God's command, Augustine opened a Bible and his eyes fell on this passage: "Not in orgies and drunkenness, not in promiscuity and licentiousness. . . . But put on the Lord Jesus Christ, and make no provision for the desires of the flesh" (Romans 13:13-14). From that moment, Augustine was freed by the Spirit to practice self-control.

Evil inclinations of all kinds appeal to us. We indulge ourselves with irritability, jealousy, gossip, pornography, and the like. We need the Spirit's grace to enable us to get these behaviors under control.

When attractive but sinful inclinations urge you to behave badly, may the Holy Spirit rush to your aid. May you ask for and receive the grace to replace self-indulgence with self-control.

Holy Spirit, Love divine, / glow within this heart of mine; / kindle every high desire; / perish self in thy pure fire. (from an 1864 hymn by Samuel Longfellow)

The Radiance of the Spirit

"You are the light of the world. . . . Your light must shine before others, that they may see your good deeds and glorify your heavenly Father."
—*Matthew 5:14, 16*

St. Basil the Great (329–378) shows how the Holy Spirit makes us a light to others:

> The Spirit raises our hearts to heaven, guides the steps of the weak, and brings to perfection those who are making progress. He enlightens those who have been cleansed from every stain of sin and makes them spiritual by communion with himself. As clear, transparent substances become very bright when sunlight falls on them and shine with a new radiance, so also souls in whom the Spirit dwells, and who are enlightened by the Spirit, become spiritual themselves and a source of grace for others.[19]

Do you consider yourself a source of light, grace, and encouragement to others? You must, because the Holy Spirit dwells in you and makes you a shining light of hope and peace. So shed every dark thought and behavior, and let your light draw others to the Lord.

May your words and actions glow with the radiance of the Spirit. May you be a beacon of good news to your family, relatives, friends— and to everyone you meet.

Let your light shine in me, O Holy Spirit. May rays of your divine light reflect your love and compassion in all of my relationships.

Everyday Courage

<>-<>-<>-<>-<>-<>-<>-<>-<>-<>-<>-<>-<>

For God did not give us a spirit of cowardice but
rather of power and love and self-control.
—2 Timothy 1:7

Fr. Emil Kapaun, a priest of the Diocese of Wichita, served selflessly as a military chaplain during the Korean War. He often went for weeks with little sleep. He ministered to the dying while providing the sacraments and encouragement to his brother soldiers, who were constantly under fire. Fr. Kapaun celebrated Mass from the hood of a jeep, and when the jeep was blown up, from the back of a bicycle. He was captured in November 1950 and sent to a prison camp, where he continued his courageous service. Fr. Kapaun buried the dead, dug latrines, gave his food to others, smuggled anti-dysentery drugs to medics, mediated disputes, and more. He died in May 1951 of a blood clot in his leg. Because of his saintly courage, Fr. Emil Kapaun is a Servant of God and on his way to canonization.

You may never face the terrors of war or captivity, but every day you experience trials, suffering and fears. Like me, you need to rely on the power and love and self-control that emboldened Fr. Emil Kapaun and that you received from the Holy Spirit in Baptism and Confirmation.

When trouble comes, may you imitate the courage of Fr. Emil Kapaun and use your spiritual power to pass through it gracefully.

O Holy Spirit, activate in me today and every day your gift of fortitude. May you strengthen me to face every challenge.

A Gift of Fear

The spirit of the Lord shall rest upon him: . . . /
a spirit of knowledge and of fear of the Lord.
—Isaiah 11:2

About a dozen years ago, I noticed that my spiritual life was doing somewhat better than usual. I took stock and observed that one thing I was doing differently was praying the Sign of the Cross more reverently. Reverence, or fear of the Lord, comes to us as one of the Spirit's seven gifts. I believe that the Holy Spirit was prompting me to sign myself more attentively. He gave me a gift of reverence to open me more fully to the graces that this great prayer and practice make available. The Spirit was also teaching me how gestures express reverence to the Lord. So I learned the importance of standing, kneeling, bowing, folding my hands, and raising my arms as ways of expressing awe in God's presence.

The Holy Spirit gave you fear of the Lord at your Confirmation. This gift does not mean cowering before the Lord in terror. Rather, it forms us in the ways of showing reverence to God. So we come before the Lord awestruck at his greatness, and express our respect by our posture and conduct.

May you exercise your spiritual gift of fear of the Lord in your thoughts, in your words, and in your actions. Awestruck at the majesty of God, may you address him in prayer and worship ever more reverently.

Come, Holy Spirit. Renew in me the gift of reverence so that I may express my awe at your greatness in my thoughts, words, and actions.

A Kiss of Kindness

Be kind to one another.
—Ephesians 4:32

Sr. Mary Victoria, a novice in a convent in Florence, Italy, was tormented with a chronic toothache. The affliction was so serious that her superiors wondered whether they should even accept her into the convent on a permanent basis. One day during a meal, Mary Victoria was quivering with pain. Moved by pity, St. Theresa Margaret of the Sacred Heart (1747–1770) leaned over and kissed her on the cheek. Immediately, Mary Victoria was free of the pain that had plagued her. The toothache never recurred, and the young woman became a regular member of the community. The Carmelite rule forbade one sister to kiss another, but Theresa Margaret wasn't thinking about rules that day. She was prompted by the Spirit to perform a small act of love, and that led to a gesture of kindness, and that led to a miracle.

The English writer Henry James once said, "Three things in human life are important: the first is to be kind; the second is to be kind; and the third is to be kind." James apparently repeated the biblical advice three times because he knew how hard it is to always be kind. Like St. Theresa Margaret, we should let the Spirit lead us to little acts of kindness—and then watch for miracles.

When your feelings tell you to be distant, cold, or even mean, may you decide to do the loving thing and behave kindly to others.

O Holy Spirit, flood me with your warmth and compassion. Prompt in me a desire always to relate to others in kindness.

The Four Essential Keys

The fruit of the Spirit is . . . faithfulness.
—Galatians 5:22

The Cursillo weekend affected me profoundly. The three-day experience of community, spontaneous prayer, expressed affection, and personal witness drew me closer to Christ. But the biggest influence on me was the Spirit-inspired teaching. The presentation titled "Piety," in particular, has oriented my life for the past five decades. The speaker taught that the Holy Spirit is the power that drives our Christian life. He explained that regular prayer, Scripture study, community, and service/evangelization are our four essential responses to his grace. If we always perform these spiritual disciplines simultaneously and faithfully, we will live lives led by the Spirit. So to my great benefit, for fifty years I have shaped my life with these four keys.

If, like me, you want to live a fruitful Christian life, one that is pleasing to the Lord, consider how you might introduce or renew these four key disciplines in your life. What would it take to assure that you perform each of them regularly?

May you perform the key disciplines with faithfulness so that you may be led and empowered by the Holy Spirit. May he draw you ever closer to the Lord Jesus and make you fruitful beyond your imagining.

O Holy Spirit, I don't want to stop trying to be faithful at daily prayer and the other spiritual disciplines. I ask you to give me the grace and strength to persevere in performing them.

Using Your Gifts Wisely

◇◇◇◇◇◇◇◇◇◇◇◇◇◇◇◇◇◇◇◇◇◇◇◇◇◇◇◇◇◇◇

*As each one has received a gift, use it to serve one
another as good stewards of God's varied grace.*
—*1 Peter 4:10*

St. Paul teaches us how to exercise the gifts of the
Holy Spirit:

Never pride yourself on being better than you
really are, but think of yourself dispassionately,
recognizing that God has given to each one his
measure of faith. . . . Then since the gifts that
we have differ according to the grace that was
given to each of us: if it is a gift of prophecy, we
should prophesy as much as our faith tells us;
if it is a gift of practical service, let us devote
ourselves to serving; if it is teaching, to teaching; if it is encouraging, to encouraging. When
you give, you should give generously from the
heart; if you are put in charge, you must be

conscientious; if you do works of mercy, let it be because you enjoy doing them. Let love be without any pretence. (Romans 12:3, 6-9; NJB)

You may recognize and use your spiritual gifts. If so, you should ask if you are using them well, and consider using them more and to greater effect. If you are not aware of your gifts, you should ask the Holy Spirit to point them out in the ways that you serve your family, your parish, your neighborhood, and your workplace.

May you discover and exercise your spiritual gifts with faith, wisdom, and humility.

O Holy Spirit, empower me with your spiritual gifts. As the Lord's disciple, grant that I might use them well and effectively.

Humility's Fruit

◇◇◇◇◇◇◇◇◇◇◇◇◇◇◇◇◇◇◇◇◇◇◇◇◇◇◇

Put on then, as God's chosen ones, . . . humility.
—Colossians 3:12

Venerable Solanus Casey (1870–1957) barely made it through the Capuchin seminary. He was ordained a "simplex priest," which limited his ministry to celebrating Mass. Fr. Solanus embraced this situation—which might have caused a lesser man to bolt in anger—and his Spirit-inspired humility bore great fruit. For forty years he served as the doorkeeper of St. Bonaventure Monastery in Detroit, Michigan, where thousands came to him for spiritual counsel. Thousands also received divine healing through his ministry. So many were cured of physical and psychological ailments that Solanus Casey ranks among the most prodigious wonder-workers in Church history. I cannot resist speculating that he touched so many lives because in humility he took the lowest place of service.

True humility requires us to see ourselves as we are and to make an accurate assessment of our gifts. To make our way in life and find our service in the body of Christ, we need the guidance of the Holy Spirit and the inspiration and wisdom of mature Christian friends.

> May the Lord surround you with Spirit-led sisters and brothers to advise and encourage you. May the Holy Spirit prevent you from thinking about yourself more highly than you ought to think, but enable you to think with sober judgment, according to the measure of faith that God has given you (cf. Romans 12:3.)

O Holy Spirit, I present myself to you as your servant and as the servant of others. By your grace, may putting others first and caring for them train me in humility and make me truly humble.

Lifelong Learning

The spirit of the LORD *shall rest upon him: /*
a spirit of . . . understanding.
—Isaiah 11:2

During my sophomore year in college, I picked up a book entitled *Of Sacraments and Sacrifice* by Fr. Clifford Howell, SJ. As I read it, I felt as though the author were strolling through my darkened mind, flipping on the lights. As a nineteen-year-old cradle Catholic, you would think I would have understood the sacraments. But Fr. Howell revealed truths that expanded my knowledge about them and opened me more fully to the flow of their graces. He taught me how the sacraments worked to bring me into contact with Christ's eternal sacrifice, how they involved me in Christ's ministry, and how they drew me nearer to him. Five decades later, I still approach the sacraments with the faith and understanding the Spirit awakened in me through Fr. Howell.

As a Christian, I regard myself as a lifelong learner, and I look to the Holy Spirit as my teacher. You should do the same. You should ask him to open the Scriptures to you and help you better understand the truths of the faith.

May you come to know Jesus more and to understand his teaching and his ways. May your growing understanding lead you to love him all the more.

Come, Holy Spirit. Bring me your gift of understanding. Flood my mind and heart with your light, and drive away the double darkness of my sin and ignorance.

The Loop of Grace

◇◇◇◇◇◇◇◇◇◇◇◇◇◇◇◇◇◇◇◇◇◇◇◇◇◇◇◇◇◇◇

I was . . . ill and you cared for me.
—Matthew 25:35-36

For more than a year, my neighbor Ron suffered at home, afflicted with the last fatal stages of chronic obstructive pulmonary disease. Ron's adult children visited when they could, and he had caretakers, but he tried to do many things for himself. One day I saw a very weak and shaking Ron struggling with an oxygen tank to get into his car. I asked where he was going. He said he was going to "try to go to the store to buy a light bulb." Observing that he might die in the attempt, I bought the bulb for him. That day I sensed the Holy Spirit prompting me to become Ron's friend and serve him. So I visited him frequently, ran errands for him, read Scripture with him, and prayed for him. The Lord blessed Ron in our friendship but blessed me even more. I gave a little of myself, and the Holy Spirit magnified my gift for both Ron and me.

Author and evangelist Fr. Robert Barron teaches about "the loop of grace." He says we give what we can to the Lord and others, and the Lord magnifies it and gives it back for us to give again. So we should invest heavily in grace by giving ourselves in service to others.

May the Holy Spirit sharpen your awareness of the needs of others close to you. May he reward you with every spiritual blessing for your loving service.

Come, Holy Spirit. Fill my heart with compassion for the poor, marginalized, sick, and imprisoned. Guide and strengthen me to serve the person in my life most in need of care.

Living Sacrifices

∞∞∞∞∞∞∞∞∞∞∞∞∞∞∞∞∞∞∞

I urge you therefore, brothers, by the mercies of God, to offer your bodies as a living sacrifice, holy and pleasing to God, your spiritual worship.
—Romans 12:1

In 1956, several Auca men, members of a primitive tribe in Ecuador, killed Jim Elliot and four other missionaries who had planned to evangelize them. Led, I believe, by the Spirit, Jim's wife, Elisabeth, forgave his killers and prayed for an opportunity to continue his mission to the Aucas. Two years later, several Auca women invited her to come to the settlement where Jim's killers lived. Elisabeth, her daughter, and another woman moved to the village. The two women, both linguists, devoted themselves to translating the New Testament into the native language and taught the Aucas about the Lord. Many of the tribe converted to Christ, including six who had martyred the missionaries. At one point, Elisabeth was reconciled with the tribesman who had killed Jim. As a sign of the reconciliation, he gave her his spear, which she keeps as a cherished memento in her home.

We all have enemies, ranging from people who offend us to people who have harmed or even killed our loved ones. To forgive such offenders, we need the mercy of God and the leadings of the Holy Spirit. And forgive we must, just as Elisabeth and Jesus did.

> May you have the grace to live each day as a living sacrifice, pouring out your life in loving service to all, even to those who have hurt you.

Come, Holy Spirit. Strengthen me with your gifts, and enable me to do the loving thing in all circumstances. As my spiritual worship, I want to serve others, especially those who have offended me.

Keeping the Peace

The fruit of the Spirit is . . . peace.
—Galatians 5:22

A model laywoman, Blessed Anne Mary Taigi (1769–1837), managed a large household in Rome for five decades. She handled the finances on a small budget and patiently cared for a large extended family. She also took in her difficult parents and her widowed daughter, Sophie, with her six children.

Her husband, Domenico, often disrupted the family with his violent temper, but Anne Mary was always able to calm him and restore peaceful relationships. In his old age, Domenico gave this touching tribute to his wife: "With her wonderful tact, she was able to maintain a heavenly peace in our home. And that, even though we were a large household full of people with very different temperaments. . . . I often came home tired, moody, and cross, but she always

156

succeeded in soothing and cheering me. And due to her, I corrected some of my faults."[20]

It took more than "wonderful tact" for Anne Mary to maintain a "heavenly peace" among the challenging people in her family. The Holy Spirit was at work in her, enabling her to build peaceful relationships with her husband and relatives. No matter how tactful you are, you will need the Holy Spirit to help you deal peacefully with testy people at home, work, or school.

May you always have the wisdom to rely on the Spirit to help you build peace into all of your relationships.

Come, Holy Spirit. Show me how to respond to others in ways that build peace, and give me the grace to create and maintain peaceful relationships.

Serving with Joy

As each one has received a gift, use it to
serve one another as good stewards
of God's varied grace.
—1 Peter 4:10

When you call Marie, the executive administrator of a large national ministry, you can tell that grace is at work in her. She greets you so pleasantly that in your mind's eye, you can see her smile. As you conduct business with Marie, she listens carefully, making you feel that your concerns are important, and she does it all with obvious joy. She is using her spiritual gift of administration to serve you as a good steward. St. Peter would say that Marie exercises her gift "with the strength that God supplies" (1 Peter 4:11). And she does not need to think about the care she gives. Marie lives in the Spirit, and as a disciple, his gifts just flow through her.

Each of us must use our gifts with the strength that God supplies and, like Marie, joyfully use them as good stewards to serve others in the Church and the world.

May you do your work and service with so much zeal and joy that others will sense that grace is flowing through you. May you use your gifts in ways that make others feel valuable and blessed.

Come, Holy Spirit. Give me the strength to use my gifts wisely and joyfully. May your grace flow freely through me to meet the needs of others.

Probing God's Mind

<><><><><><><><><><><><><><><><><><><><>

*No one knows what pertains to God except the
Spirit of God.*
—1 Corinthians 2:11

St. Paul explains that the Holy Spirit gives us the
mind of God:

"What no eye has seen, nor ear heard, / nor the
heart of man conceived, / what God has prepared
for those who love him," / God has revealed to us
through the Spirit. For the Spirit searches everything, even the depths of God. For what person
knows a man's thoughts except the spirit of the
man which is in him? So also no one compre-
hends the thoughts of God except the Spirit of
God. Now we have received not the spirit of the
world, but the Spirit which is from God, that we
might understand the gifts bestowed on us by
God. And we impart this in words not taught by

human wisdom but taught by the Spirit, interpreting spiritual truths to those who possess the Spirit. (1 Corinthians 2:9-13, RSV)

The Lord has arranged for us to live supernatural lives by giving us gifts that bring us as children into his divine family. If we fail to embrace the workings of the Spirit, who reveals God's mind to us, we overlook these graces and live impoverished, worldly lives.

May you become so attuned to the leadings of the Spirit that you begin to comprehend the mind of God and receive his gifts in abundance.

Come, Holy Spirit. Reveal to me your truths and your ways so that as I come to know you more, I may also love you more.

Loving Like God

The fruit of the Spirit is love.
—*Galatians 5:22*

For two decades, St. Aelred (1110–1167) served as abbot of Rievaulx in northern England, a monastery of 150 monks and 500 brothers. He demonstrated that love, as a fruit of the Spirit, is love in action. Love characterized Aelred's leadership and behavior. He ruled his community with compassion and gentleness. Unlike other medieval abbots, Aelred encouraged his men to develop relationships and express affection. He did not dismiss a single monk in his twenty years as abbot. Aelred governed with kindness, not laxity, and always found a way to help a troubled or troublesome brother. He regarded Rievaulx as a "community of love" and described it in a letter to his sister: "As I was walking round the cloisters, all the brethren sat together, . . . and in the whole of that throng, I could not find one whom I did not love, and by whom I was not loved."[21]

God loves us unconditionally and selflessly, no matter what. Deep down, all people hunger for that kind of love. Touched by the Holy Spirit, we are able to love others just as God loves us.

> May you bask in the generous and gentle love of the Lord. Transformed by his care for you, may you express your love for others without conditions and without regard to circumstances.

Come, Holy Spirit. I open my heart to you. Fill me with your love, and give me the grace to love others without conditions, without expecting any return, no matter what.

The Supreme Desire

<><><><><><><><><><><><><><><><><><><><><><>

The LORD is near to all who call upon him. /
. . . He fulfills the desire of those who fear him.
—Psalm 145:18-19

From childhood, St. Thérèse of Lisieux (1873–1897) desired to become a missionary and a martyr. It soon became clear to her, however, that neither option was open to a cloistered nun. So she sought the Holy Spirit and searched the Scriptures for another way to excel. "I was determined to find an elevator to carry me to Jesus, for I was too small to climb the steep stairs of perfection. So I sought in Holy Scripture some idea of what this lift I wanted would be, and I read, 'Whoever is a little one, let him come to me" [cf. Luke 18:16]. It is your arms, Jesus, which are the elevator to carry me to heaven."[22]

The Lord exceeded Thérèse's desires by giving her a higher calling than that of missionary or martyr. He prompted her to do everything with love, and so she became a channel of grace for others. After her death, thousands have experienced miracles that flow from her intercession.

When the Lord wanted to reward St. Thomas Aquinas (1225–1274) for what he had done and written, he asked the saint what he desired. "Only you, Lord," said Thomas. Like Thérèse and Thomas, we must set our hearts on the highest of desires—the Lord himself and his kingdom.

May you approach the Lord with reverence, and may you allow him to subsume all your desires into the supreme desire of union with him.

O Lord, my heart's desire is to know you as you know me, to love you as you love me, to serve you as you serve me, and to obey you as you obey the Father.

Prayers to the Holy Spirit

COME, HOLY SPIRIT

Come, Holy Spirit, fill the hearts of your faithful and enkindle in them the fire of your love. Send forth your Spirit and they shall be created. And you shall renew the face of the earth.

O God, who by the light of the Holy Spirit did instruct the hearts of the faithful, grant that by the same Holy Spirit, we may be truly wise and ever enjoy his consolations. Through Christ Our Lord. Amen.

Veni Creator Spiritus[23]

Come, Creator Spirit, come
from your bright heavenly throne,
come take possession of our souls,
and make them all your own.

You who are called the Paraclete,
best gift of God above,
the living spring, the vital fire,
sweet christ'ning and true love.

You who are sev'nfold in your grace,
Finger of God's right hand,
his promise, teaching all of us
to speak and understand.

O guide our minds with your blest light,
with love our hearts inflame;
and with your strength, which ne'er decays,
confirm our mortal frame.

Far from us drive our deadly foe;
true peace unto us bring;
and through all perils lead us safe
beneath your sacred wing.

Through you may we the Father know,
through you th'eternal Son,
and you the Spirit of them both,
thrice-blessed Three in One.

All glory to the Father be,
with his co-equal Son;
the same to you, great Paraclete,
while endless ages run.

Veni Sancte Spiritus[24]

Holy Spirit, font of light,
focus of God's glory bright,
shed on us a shining ray.

Father of the fatherless,
giver of gifts limitless,
come and touch our hearts today.

Source of strength and sure relief,
comforter in times of grief,
enter in and be our guest.

On our journey grant us aid,
freshening breeze and cooling shade,
in our labor inward rest.

Enter each aspiring heart,
occupy its inmost part
with your dazzling purity.

All that gives to us our worth,
all that benefits the earth,
you bring to maturity.

With your soft refreshing rains,
break our drought, remove our stains;
bind up all our injuries.

Shake with rushing wind our will;
melt with fire our icy chill;
bring to light our perjuries.

As your promise we believe,
make us ready to receive
gifts from your unbounded store.

Grant enabling energy,
courage in adversity,
joys that last forevermore.
Amen.

HOLY SPIRIT, TRUTH DIVINE[25]

Holy Spirit, Truth divine,
dawn upon this soul of mine;
Word of God and inward light,
wake my spirit, clear my sight.

Holy Spirit, Love divine,
glow within this heart of mine;
kindle every high desire;
perish self in thy pure fire.

Holy Spirit, Power divine,
fill and nerve this will of mine;
grant that I may strongly live,
bravely bear, and nobly strive.

Holy Spirit, Right divine,
King within my conscience reign;
be my Lord, and I shall be
firmly bound, forever free.

Recommended Resources

The Catechism of the Catholic Church, Second Edition, 683–747.

United States Catholic Catechism for Adults (Washington, DC: United States Conference of Catholic Bishops, 2006), chap. 9: "Receive the Holy Spirit," 101–110.

Baptism in the Holy Spirit (Locust Grove, VA: National Service Committee of the Catholic Charismatic Renewal in the United States, 2012).

George T. Montague, SM. *Holy Spirit Make Your Home in Me* (Frederick, MD: The Word Among Us Press, 2008).

George T. Montague, SM. *Mary's Life in the Spirit* (Frederick, MD: The Word Among Us Press, 2011).

As by a New Pentecost (Set of 2 DVDs)
Renewal Ministries (www.renewalministries.net

Acknowledgments

Many friends helped me with this book, some by letting me tell their stories and others by suggesting improvements to the text. I extend special thanks to Gladys Bertram, Patricia Easton, Richard Easton, Deacon Henry Libersat, Mary Martin, George Martin, Brandon Vogt and Kathleen Vogt. I am grateful to Patty Mitchell, my kind editor, for inviting me to write this book and to the entire team at The Word Among Us for their great service to me.

Endnotes

1. *On the Holy Spirit,* a treatise by St. Basil the Great (329–378), in *The Office of Readings According to the Roman Rite,* trans. the International Commission on English in the Liturgy (Boston: Daughters of St. Paul, 1983), 563.

2. F. J. Sheed, *Theology for Beginners* (Ann Arbor, MI: Servant Books, 1981), 35–36.

3. Gregory of Nyssa in *Nicene and Post-Nicene Fathers,* series II, vol. 5.

4. Quoted in Robert Claude, SJ, *The Soul of Pier-Giorgio Frassati* (New York: Spiritual Book Associates, 1960), 93.

5. *On the Holy Spirit,* a catechetical instruction by St. Cyril of Jerusalem (ca. 315–386), in *The Office of Readings According to the Roman Rite,* trans. the International Commission on English in the Liturgy (Boston: Daughters of St. Paul, 1983), 629–30.

6. The Septuagint and Vulgate translations read "piety" for "fear of the Lord" in verse 2, thus accounting for seven gifts.

7. *On the Trinity,* a treatise by St. Hilary (ca. 315–368), in *The Office of Readings According to the Roman Rite,* trans. the International Commission on English in the Liturgy (Boston: Daughters of St. Paul, 1983), 640.

8. St. Jane Frances de Chantal, Conference 30, "On the Excellence of Prayer," *Her Exhortations, Conferences,*

Instructions, and Retreat (Clifton: E. Austin & Sons, 1888), 206–7.

9. The English translation of the Order of the Mass from *The Roman Missal* © 2010. International Commission on English in the Liturgy.

10. Adapted from a text by George Guitton, SJ, *Perfect Friend: The Life of Blessed Claude La Columbière* (St. Louis, Missouri: B. Herder Book Co., © 1956), 324.

11. The Septuagint and Vulgate translations read "piety" for "fear of the Lord" in verse 2, thus accounting for seven gifts.

12. Benedict XV, *General Audience*, May 23, 2012.

13. St. Thomas, *Emitte Spiritum*, Sermon for Pentecost, accessed at http://dhspriory.org/thomas/Serm11Emitte. htm, consulted October 10, 2012.

14. C. S. Lewis, *The Weight of Glory and Other Addresses* (New York: The Macmillan Company, 1949), 15.

15. George T. Montague, SM, *Holy Spirit, Make Your Home in Me* (Frederick, MD: The Word Among Us Press, 2008), 182.

16. St. Irenaeus, *Against Heresies* (Book 3:17, 1–32), in *The Office of Readings According to the Roman Rite,* trans. the International Commission on English in the Liturgy (Boston: Daughters of St. Paul, 1983), 648.

17. George T. Montague, SM, *Mary's Life in the Spirit* (Frederick, MD: The Word Among Us Press, 2011), 108.

18. George T. Montague, SM, *Holy Spirit, Make Your Home in Me*, 131, 133.

19. *On the Holy Spirit*, a treatise by St. Basil the Great (329–378), in *The Office of Readings According to the Roman Rite*, trans. the International Commission on English in the Liturgy (Boston: Daughters of St. Paul, 1983), 632.

20. *Voices of the Saints*, Bert Ghezzi (New York: Double-day Image Books, 2000).

21. *Butler's Lives of the Saints: New Full Edition*, ed. David Hugh Farmer (Collegeville, MN: The Liturgical Press, 1995–2000, 12 vols.), January, 82.

22. *The Autobiography of Saint Thérèse of Lisieux: The Story of a Soul*, trans. John Beevers (New York: Doubleday Image Books, 1989), 113–14.

23. Attributed to Rabanus Maurus (776–876), adapted from *Liturgy of the Hours*, trans. anon. (New York: Catholic Book Publishing Company, 1976), II, 1–11.

24. Archbishop Stephen Langton of Canterbury (ca. 1150–1228), *Veni Sancte Spiritus*, trans. Rev. Dr. John Webster Grant, *The Hymnbook of the Anglican Church of Canada and the United Church of Canada* (Toronto: Cooper and Beatty, 1971), no. 248. Used by permission of Phyllis Airhart, copyright holder, for the translation of the *Veni Sancte Spiritus*.

25. Samuel Longfellow (1819–1892), *Holy Spirit, Truth Divine*, accessed at https://nethymnal.org/htm/h/o/holstdiv.htm, consulted January 6, 2014.